THE ETERNAL GOSPEL FOR THE WEARY SOUL

Elizabeth Viera Talbot

Pacific Press®
Publishing Association

Nampa, Idaho | Oshawa, Ontario, Canada
www.pacificpress.com

Cover design by Steve Lanto
Cover art by Morgan Weistling
Interior design by Aaron Troia
Outside editor: Aivars Ozolins, PhD

Copyright © 2015 by Pacific Press® Publishing Association
Printed in the United States of America
All rights reserved

The author assumes full responsibility for the accuracy of all facts and quotations as cited in this book.

You can obtain additional copies of this book by calling toll-free 1-800-765-6955 or by visiting http://www.adventistbookcenter.com.

ISBN 13: 978-0-8163-5841-0
ISBN 10: 0-8163-5841-9

May 2015

Dedication

I dedicate this book to my beloved mother, Alicia Meier de Viera, who is *resting* in Christ until the resurrection morning, when His sweet voice will be calling her to an eternal life of *rest*.

And to Jesus, my Savior and Redeemer, who has given me a complete *rest* for my soul now, while I am still alive. May this book bring Him glory and honor, and may it lead weary souls to the cross, where they may enter *His True Rest*.

"Come to Me, all who are weary and heavy-laden, and **I WILL GIVE YOU REST.** Take My yoke upon you and learn from Me, for I am gentle and humble in heart, and *YOU WILL FIND REST FOR YOUR SOULS.* For My yoke is easy and My burden is light."

—Matthew 11:28–30

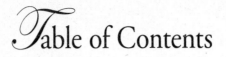

Table of Contents

CHAPTER 1

REST in Jesus' VICTORY!!

This was an experience that defies explanation. A profound realization took over my whole being as I stood by my mother's hospital bed a few hours before she passed away. Her journey was about to end, seven years after the first cancer diagnosis. She had prepared herself well for this moment and had the most positive and grateful spirit that I have ever witnessed. She was dying with the full assurance of her salvation in Jesus, and therefore her soul was filled with peace beyond understanding. Her attitude was such a gift to all of us who love her dearly, because she kept referring to her impending death as just a *"siesta,"* a little nap, until she wakes up to see the face of Jesus at the Second Coming.

As I contemplated her beautiful and sweet face, which was filled with an expression of rest and peace, I also noticed her shallow breathing and realized that the time she had left on this earth was very short. Suddenly, every biblical doctrine that I had ever believed, studied, or taught; all the stories from Genesis to Revelation; the entire plan of salvation through the life, death, and resurrection of Jesus as explained in the Scriptures; seemed to be swallowed up by a gigantic funnel that resulted in one single core belief that was either **all** true or it wasn't. At that moment, there was room for only **one final reality**:

- She had been saved through Jesus, or she had not.
- Either I would see my mom again, or I wouldn't.
- Either Jesus wins, or He doesn't.

That simple. That profound. That **real**!

In the midst of this very personal and yet cosmic realization, I watched her take her final breath and, in that one instant, cease to be a living soul. At that moment, one reality trumped all my other thoughts, feelings, and beliefs: She was resting in Jesus; evil could no longer touch her, pain could no longer reach her, the devil could no longer bother her. She was in complete *rest* in Jesus.

She was in complete rest in Jesus.

And that was true not merely because she had died, but because she had passed away with the full assurance of her eternal salvation in Jesus' salvific work on her behalf. The truth was that she had entered God's True Rest long before she died! She ceased her life with a *"sabbathed* soul," as described in Hebrews 4:9–11: "So there remains a Sabbath rest for the people of God. For the one who has entered *His rest* has himself also *rested* from his works, as God did from His. There-fore let us be diligent to enter *that rest*" (emphasis added).

I turned to Facebook to share my mother's passing with our family, friends, and prayer and ministry

> *W*e better have a clear, unquestionable, and assured reality: *rest in Jesus*, because **Jesus wins!**

partners. And yet I could not post the news without the reminder of this **one** ultimate reality. My post was accompanied by a triumphant two-word cry: **Jesus wins!** This headline became the title of my homily that I gave a few weeks later at her memorial service.

When the rubber meets the road, when we are at our wit's end, when we come to the end of our journey, or when the life of a loved one is about to slip away, we better have a clear, unquestionable, and assured reality: *rest in Jesus,* because **Jesus wins!**

It's all about Jesus!!

In one of the most fascinating chapters of the Bible, two men, who also are mourning the loss of a loved one, discuss the baffling events of the previous two days as they walk toward a town called Emmaus. They have a great many questions and yet no answers. Their hopes have been shattered by their helplessness in the face of cruel reality. All that they have ever believed in seems to have been swallowed up by a gigantic black hole of hopelessness, leaving them in complete darkness and despair.

In the midst of their confusion, they are suddenly joined by the resurrected Jesus, even though they don't recognize Him. They try to explain to the "stranger" that up until two days ago they had strong religious beliefs and convictions, which are entirely useless now. Were the Law and the prophets not true? How could the Messiah die? Had they really believed in a lie? How will their hearts ever be able to believe again?

And in the midst of their despair, Jesus decides to help them see something very important, something crucial: all the Scriptures were written to convey **one core reality.** "And He said to them, 'O foolish men and slow of heart to believe in all that the prophets have spoken! Was it not necessary for the Christ to suffer these things and to enter into His glory?' *Then beginning with Moses and with all the prophets He explained to them the things concerning Himself in all the Scriptures*" (Luke 24:25–27; emphasis added).

Jesus had joined them in order to funnel all of their understanding of doctrines and teachings of the Law and the prophets, all of their religious concepts, into one single reality called the "gospel" or the "good news," and to explain to them that all these teachings pointed to that **one** reality: Himself! For those of you who like the original words in Greek, the verb used for "to explain" in verse 27 is *diermeneuō*. The English word *hermeneutics*, which is used in academic circles in reference to the methodology of interpreting biblical texts, is part of this Greek word. Jesus, in fact, is offering them a fascinating and exciting theology class, remind-

Everything was pointing to Jesus!

ing them that they need to start from the beginning: everything they ever read and believed from the Jewish Scriptures, from Genesis on, was pointing to Jesus' death and resurrection. Yes! Every Sabbath celebration, every Day of Atonement, every service in the sanctuary, every annual Passover Feast, every jubilee, everything was pointing to **Jesus**!

Aside from the bewildered looks on their faces, something unprecedented happened to them. An untamable Woo-hoo!—the type that is bursting at its seams—was born in their hearts! And the same two men, who moments before had been overtaken by their darkest fears, now had their hearts burning with uncontainable joy in the light of this new understanding! They had to go back; they had to tell the others who were still mourning that their hopes and beliefs had not been swallowed up by a black hole of hopelessness and despair but instead had been purged and reinterpreted by the hermeneutical funnel of the eternal *gospel*: **Jesus wins!**

"They said to one another, 'Were not our *hearts burning* within us while He was speaking to us on the road, *while He was explaining [diermeneuō] the Scriptures* to us?' And they got up that very hour and returned to Jerusalem" (Luke 24:32, 33; emphasis added). They had to share the eternal gospel because their tears had been turned into a "mega joy" (see Luke 24:52; "great" from the Greek *mega*).

Jesus thought this **one core reality** was extremely important! He had to deliver it *personally* to the rest of the disciples when all of them were gathered together. Jesus knew that human beings have a tendency to forget the *real* meaning of religious forms, commandments, traditions, and symbols and are always in danger of worshiping the forms and not the reality they point to. That is why He made a point to remind all of His disciples that *everything* in the Jewish Scriptures was about Him. But before we go to the second announcement of Jesus, let me share with you a fascinating little story.

Jesus thought this one core reality was extremely important!

Understanding with "open" minds

Bob Atchison, a man fascinated with the Alexander Palace in Russia, shared an amusing and yet insightful anecdote. "For generations before Alexandra [the last Russian empress], the Russian Imperial family had loved flowers. Catherine the Great treasured her roses in Tsarskoye Selo and had special guards assigned to protect them year-round from the harsh climate and accidents. Once an Imperial order had been given, it was followed until rescinded. Over a century after Catherine died, Nicholas and Alexandra discovered a guard still stationed to protect a long vanished rose of Catherine's."[1]

Can you imagine that? Imperial guards, just standing there in the middle of nowhere for more than one hundred years, guarding a rosebush that no longer existed, just because there had been an imperial order to do so many years before? As the years went by, everyone had forgotten why; therefore, the guard would stand there, guarding nothing—just because that's the way it was supposed to be by imperial order.

Jesus wanted to make sure that this did not happen to His disciples and the Christian church. From the very beginning, Jesus wanted His church to understand that all the Jewish Scriptures that we call the Old Testament were about Him. He realized that many were keeping a *Sabbath day of rest* but were rejecting Him. (They were just standing there, guarding a tradition while at the same time rejecting the **real Rose** of Sharon!) Others kept talking about Sabbath laws and making the day a burden instead of a feast of remembrance of their creation and redemption. He understood that even though He had died on the Passover Friday, very few had realized that He had been the real Passover Lamb (1 Corinthians 5:7), whose blood would protect everyone who believed from judgment! So, on resurrection day, He made a second appearance, this time to all the disciples, and personally explained the Scriptures to them: "Now He said to them, 'These are My words which I spoke to you while I was still with you, that all things which are written about Me in the Law of Moses and the Prophets and the Psalms must be fulfilled.' Then *He opened their minds to understand the Scriptures*" (Luke 24: 44, 45; emphasis added).

He didn't want His church to merely believe in a disjointed jumble of doctrines, stories, traditions, and beliefs floating in a sea of ignorance.

He opened their minds! The same Greek verb meaning "to open" was used by Luke in the narratives about Jesus "opening" the ears of the deaf and the eyes of the blind. But now, He "opened their minds"! He didn't want His church to merely believe in a disjointed jumble of doctrines, stories, traditions, and beliefs floating in a sea of ignorance. He knew that the winds of strife would come and that, at times, their journey would take them into the valley of death, and that during those times of extreme crisis they would discover that, all these things they had believed in, would tend to be swallowed up into a big black hole—unless they understood that Jesus, and Him crucified, was the **one core reality** that all these others pointed to. Only then would they *rest* in Him, no matter what.

Developmental understanding

In His mercy, God has explained the plan of redemption throughout the Bible in a developmental manner. Redemptive history contains multiple fulfillments of events and prophecies because God has been revealing the plan of salvation in a progressive and developmental way throughout the history of Israel and the world. God has been speaking since the very beginning, and yet we can understand the full meaning of each story, doctrine, and commandment **only** when we study it in the light of the cross. The author of Hebrews starts his book by highlighting the developmental dimension of God's revelation, fully manifested through Christ: "God, after He spoke long ago to the fathers in the prophets in many portions and in many ways, in these last days has spoken to us in His Son, whom He appointed heir of all things, through whom also He made the world. And He is the radiance of His glory and the exact representation of His nature" (Hebrews 1:1–3).

Only Jesus, and Him crucified, is the whole substance, everything else points to Him! An easy way to understand this principle is to visualize the whole Bible as a developmental graphic that finds its fulfillment and maximum expansion at the cross:

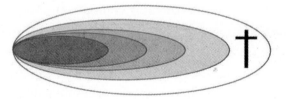

One of my favorite authors of all times explains this principle very eloquently: "The sacrifice of Christ as an atonement for sin is *the great truth* around which all other truths cluster. In order to be rightly understood and appreciated, every truth in the word of God, from Genesis to Revelation, must be studied in the light that streams from the cross of Calvary. I present before you the great, grand monument of mercy and regeneration, salvation and redemption,—the Son of God uplifted on the cross. *This is to be the foundation of every discourse given by our ministers.*"[2] There it is! The sacrifice of Christ as atonement for sin is the great truth around which all other truths cluster, and it must be the foundation of every single sermon preached, every class taught, and every discourse given.

Most believers have applied this understanding to a few themes in the Bible but not to all doctrines and commandments. For example, most Bible students have been able to identify multiple fulfillments for the Passover: first in Egypt (Exodus 12–14), when all the people of Israel understood that the blood of the Passover lamb on the doorposts kept them safe from the angel of judgment. Later on, we find Israel taking the Passover as a reminder of God's deliverance, and they take it before crossing to conquer the Promised Land and Jericho. As the meaning develops in the New Testament, we find Jesus dying on Passover Friday, at the time of the Passover sacrifice. Paul then makes it clear for all of us: "For Christ our Passover also has been sacrificed" (1 Corinthians 5:7). And hopefully everyone understands that "therefore there is now no condemnation for those who are in Christ Jesus" (Romans 8:1).

And yet I am saddened and puzzled when a Christian explains such doctrines as the *Sabbath day of rest*, the Day of Atonement, paradise, the state of the dead, end-time prophecies, or any other Bible truth without understanding these in the light of the cross. I have watched countless people become tired and weary of rule after rule, commandment after commandment, chart after chart, and prophecy after prophecy, without understanding these in Christ, and therefore they live their religious lives in constant anxiety with a schizophrenic theology. They say something like, "Yes, of course we are saved by Jesus, but . . ." and then proceed to add many other requirements. As Max Lucado insightfully observes, when discussing Peter's sermon in Acts 2:

> No more striving after God's approval. "You can rest now," he told them.
>
> And they did. For about fourteen pages, which in my Bible is the distance between the sermon of Peter in Acts 2 and the meeting of the church in Acts 15. In the first, grace was preached. In the second, grace was questioned. It wasn't that the people didn't believe in grace at all. They did. *They believed in grace a lot. They just didn't believe in*

grace alone. They wanted to add to the work of Christ.

Grace-a-lots believe in grace, a lot. Jesus almost finished the work of salvation, they argue. In the rowboat named *Heaven Bound,* Jesus paddles most of the time. But every so often he needs our help. So we give it.[3]

Rest already!

In spite of God's best efforts, throughout human history we keep having this misplaced zeal to worship the symbol and reject its substance, its true meaning, the core reality it points to. It happened to the Israelites, who were saved from sure death—venomous snakes—when God designed a very unusual antidote that pointed to the ultimate reality of Jesus' death.

"Then the LORD said to Moses, 'Make a fiery serpent, and set it on a standard, and it shall come about, that everyone who is bitten, when he looks at it, he will live.' And Moses made a bronze serpent and set it on the standard; and it came about, that if a serpent bit any man, when he looked to the bronze serpent, he lived" (Numbers 21:8, 9).

Guess what happened after some years went by? Israel started worshiping that bronze serpent as if it had some kind of magical powers, instead of worshiping the God who gave them that reminder of His salvific power. Therefore, eventually King Hezekiah had to destroy the bronze serpent to stop that kind of idolatrous worship! "He removed the high places and broke down the sacred pillars and cut down the Asherah. He also broke in pieces *the bronze serpent that Moses had made, for until those days the sons of Israel burned incense to it*" (2 Kings 18:4; emphasis added). Can you imagine? Worshiping the symbol in place of the Lord of the symbol!

This is exactly what Stephen was preaching in front of the high priest when the religious people stoned him to death and he became the first Christian martyr. He told them that they had become as idolatrous as those who worshiped the golden calf and brought sacrifices to an idol made with their hands (read Stephen's fascinating sermon in Acts 7). Now they had the temple but were rejecting the Lord of the temple; they were resisting Him whom the temple services and sacrifices pointed to.

In the same manner, in the topic of the weekly Sabbath rest, which was supposed to point us to the complete *rest* in the reality that our Creator is also our Redeemer, I found that many were worshiping the Sabbath while rejecting the complete gospel of the Lord of the Sabbath. Like imperial guards, they were standing by rose-free dry ground, not sure why, but with an imperial order to do so. Instead of a feast of remembrance and celebration of our redemption, many were trying to make this day a ladder to climb in order to reach heaven. And so it happened that after years of observing church members with long faces, constantly looking at their watches to know the exact time of sunset when the Sabbath would be over and making joyless and never-ending lists of what you could or couldn't do on this holy day, I decided to research the topic of *true rest in Christ*. And that is how my PhD dissertation was conceived.

> *Instead of a feast of remembrance and celebration of our redemption, many were trying to make this day a ladder to climb in order to reach heaven.*

I was especially interested in the well-known passage found in Matthew 11:28–30: "Come to Me, all who are weary and heavy-laden, and I will give you *rest*. Take My yoke upon you and learn from Me, for I am gentle and humble in heart, and YOU WILL FIND REST FOR YOUR SOULS. For My yoke is easy and My burden is light" (emphasis added).

I was particularly intrigued by the fact that these verses are immediately followed by the only two stories in Matthew's Gospel that take place on the Sabbath (Matthew 12:1–8; 9–14). Moreover, Jesus is questioned about not keeping the Sabbath appropriately! Within a few verses, Jesus declares Himself the *Provider of rest* (Matthew 11:28–30) and the *Lord of the Sabbath* (Matthew 12:8).

So what did this mean for the Matthean Jewish-Christian community that was starting to interpret the Law and the prophets in the light of the cross? Were they carrying heavy burdens that Jesus never intended for them to carry (see Matthew 23:4)? I spent many, many years researching this amazing topic, and now I am so excited to share it with you! And I pray that the content of this book, under the influence of the Holy Spirit, will open our minds to understand the importance of our rest in Christ, and how, when discovered, it leads to unprecedented freedom and uncontainable joy and celebration.

> *And I was, and continue to be, at rest in Christ, because I believe in the eternal gospel for the weary soul.*

* * * * *

And there I was, standing by the lifeless body of my beloved mom, and then it dawned on me that, in fact, we both were at *rest*! She had died in the full assurance of her salvation in Jesus and was taking a little *"siesta"* now until

Rest in Jesus' Victory!!

Christ would come to awaken her. And I was, and continue to be, at *rest* in Christ, because I believe in the eternal gospel for the weary soul. I trust with all my heart, mind, body, and soul (with all the doctrines, commandments, and prophecies intact) that I can *rest* from my works in Christ's sufficiency, in His accomplished work at the cross that gives me the assurance of eternal life. Vehemently, through this book, I want to extend an invitation to you too: **rest already!! Jesus wins!!**

1. Bob Atchison, "A Romanov Passion for Flowers," Alexander Palace Time Machine, accessed May 20, 2015, http://www.alexanderpalace.org/palace/blog.html?pid=1213306016379451.

2. Ellen G. White, *Gospel Workers* (Washington, DC: Review and Herald® Publishing Association, 1915), 315; emphasis added.

3. Max Lucado, *Grace: More Than We Deserve, Greater Than We Imagine* (Nashville, TN: Thomas Nelson, 2012), 45; emphasis added.

Chapter 2

ℛEST in Jesus' FAITHFULNESS!!

Several years ago I wrote a book titled *Surprised by Love,* published by Pacific Press®. In this book, I share one of the most dramatic events of my childhood, and I would like to start this chapter by revisiting that story.[1] We were in the Argentinian Patagonia because my dad was an evangelist and the three of us (Dad, Mom, and I) used to move to a new location about every six months. I was four years old, and one sunny afternoon my mother had decided to take me for a ride.

We lived in a very small house, made of mud. There was not much for me to do at home, so my mother borrowed a bicycle to take me for a fun sightseeing ride. I was so excited! I was not old enough to ride this bike myself, so I settled in a small seat behind my mother. She was the one in charge, pedaling and steering our tour; I was the one enjoying it in the back. So we began. We had been going for quite a while and were now far away from the town, enjoying the never-ending wheat fields. At one point on a particularly bumpy part of the road I started to slide sideways off of the bike seat. My mother advised me to straighten up and to hold on firmly, so I wouldn't fall. And I did. And a nightmare began. I started crying with utter desperation, and my mom couldn't understand why. She stopped the bike and asked me why I was crying. I was unable to talk because of severe pain. What was happening? She couldn't see anything wrong, but I kept pointing to my feet. I had socks that covered my legs almost up to my knees, and my mom decided she had to take my socks off to find out what was going on. So she did. And then she saw it!! The flesh at the bottom of my foot came off along with the sock, and she could see a white bone where my heel and my foot used to be. As I had tried to straighten up on the seat, I had accidentally stuck my foot in the moving wheel, which had completely destroyed my foot. We were miles away from the little town we lived in, and even if we were there, they did not have adequate medical facilities to deal with something of this magnitude. Plus, I couldn't move and was bleeding so heavily that my mom was afraid that I would bleed to death in no time, right there, in the middle of nowhere.

Well, my mother didn't have to think about it twice. With energy and strength that came directly from heaven, my mom sat me on the main seat of the bicycle and took hold of the handlebars and started to run to take me back to town. I don't know how she ran all those miles or how she kept herself together. All she knew was that she needed to do for me what I couldn't do for myself. Save me. After all, I was her little girl! It turned out that I had no broken bones; but even so, it took me about six months to walk again. There is a tiny little scar on my heel that reminds me of that fateful day. The day when

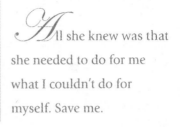

All she knew was that she needed to do for me what I couldn't do for myself. Save me.

my mom also became my rescuer, because she did for me what I couldn't do for myself. She ran for me because I had become handicapped; my feet could not run nor pedal, so she used her feet to carry me. My mother had given me life in the first place when I was born, and now she had given me life all over again because she had rescued me from certain death.

The reason why I wanted to revisit this story is to remind you that this is how parents naturally respond when their child is in trouble. At no point did I fear that she would leave me there in the wheat fields without doing everything she possibly could to save my life. I was *so* assured of her love for me that my little heart could *rest* in her ability to rescue me when I could do absolutely nothing for myself.

It seems that the moment your child is born you make

an instant tacit covenant with your baby. No matter what happens to your children or what decisions they make, they will never stop being your children. You may end up having an ex-spouse, but you will never have an ex-child! Your children will always be your children and your greatest treasure. From birth, loving parents constantly assure their children of their love and commitment in so many ways: songs and kisses, tucking them into bed and reading stories, providing encouragement and celebrating not only their birthdays but also every small step and achievement.

When God created us, the same thing happened to Him! Throughout the Bible, He tells us that He is the one who brought us into life and that He did not abandon us when we became handicapped by sin! No! No! On the contrary, He sends us constant reminders about His covenant to redeem us and to re-create us! And one of those reminders—that we can rest in His faithfulness—is a weekly *rest* celebration that He set apart for human beings from the beginning! "The Sabbath was made for man, and not man for the Sabbath" (Mark 2:27). So let's start there, shall we?

And God shouted: Very good!

Take a moment to read the Creation narrative in Genesis 1 and 2. The Bible starts with, "In the beginning

God created the heavens and the earth" (Genesis 1:1). These seven Hebrew words that make up the first sentence in the Scriptures foreshadow the seven days of the creation process. After a detailed account of the first five days of Creation, the narrative clearly and repeatedly highlights the importance of the sixth day over the previous five days. For example, in Hebrew this is the first time the definite article "the" is used with a creation day: a first day, a second day, a third day, a fourth day, a fifth day, **the** sixth day (verse 31). *The day* has arrived!

From the second to the fifth day of Creation, we read of God's assessment of what was accomplished in each day, and it says, "it was good" (Genesis 1:10, 12, 18, 21). But on the sixth day, the goal of Creation is to be revealed and the crowning piece manifested. Of all the days of Creation week, the sixth receives the longest coverage in the narrative. There is a two-part creation in this day; in the first part, God made the living creatures, the beasts of the earth, and, once again, He assesses His work and says that "it was good" (verses 24, 25).

And then God pauses . . .

A divine counsel takes place *exclusively* for creating humankind in the Creation narrative. As God is dialoguing in community, we get a glimpse of the uniqueness and climactic significance of this moment: "Then God said, 'Let Us make man . . .' " (verse 26). "Man"

I Will Give You *Rest*

(*'adam*) is a collective name for humankind, as it will be further explained in Genesis 1:27. God has reflected and decided to have children. They would be in *His* image: "Let Us make man in Our image, according to Our likeness; and let them rule over the fish of the sea and over the birds of the sky and over the cattle and over all the earth, and over every creeping thing that creeps on the earth" (verse 26).

Humankind would bear God's image and likeness; they would be like God but not identical to God; in His image and likeness but not "gods." God had made the decision; in Genesis 1:26, we hear the voice of God in the first person. Then the narrator poetically reports the creation of God's children in the third person, emphasizing that we were created in His image: "God created man in His own image, in the image of God He created him; male and female He created them" (verse 27).

> Amazing! You and I are in the image of God!

God's children are designated by gender, not by kinds or species like the animals. He created a male *'adam* and a female *'adam*. The Creator created "procreators." Each gender was bestowed with amazing and unique characteristics for a complementary and complete representation of the image of God. Amazing! You and I are in the image of God!

Humans, and only humans in all of creation, are in God's image. The phrase "the image of God" appears only four times in the Jewish Scriptures (Genesis 1:26, 27 [twice]; 9:6), and they all relate to the creation of humankind. Later on, Adam would have a child "in his own likeness, according to his image" (Genesis 5:3). You have children in your image. Humankind is created in the image of the Sovereign Creator. They hold the highest place in the created order. Are you feeling pretty special by now?

Well, God thinks that His children are more than special. When He evaluates His creative work of the sixth day, He can't just call it "good" as in all the other days. No! The plants and the animals are good, but the children are **very good**! "God saw all that He had made, and behold, it was *very good*. And there was evening and there was morning, *the* sixth day" (Genesis 1:31; emphasis added). This was *the* day they came to life, and God would always remember it, the way you remember *the days* on which your children were born. Those are the most important days in your life! And they were *very good*!

It is completed!

Now that His children had come to life, the creation process was complete; it was done, finished, and perfect. It was time to celebrate! God ceased His work and blessed and sanctified the seventh day; the day that would forever point to the completeness and wholeness of God's creation. The seventh day would be perpetually linked with the creation and also with the redemption (recreation) of humankind. As the children of God, humans spent the very first day of their lives together with the Creator. In the special garden made for them, they celebrated the completeness of God's creation, of which they were the crowning masterpiece. The seventh day was *the* first day the Creator and His children spent together in intimate communion.

> The seventh day was *the* first day the Creator and His children spent together in intimate communion.

"By the seventh day God completed His work which He had done, and He rested on the seventh day from all His work which He had done. Then God blessed the seventh day and sanctified it, because in it He rested from all His work which God had created and made" (Genesis 2:2, 3).

The Creator and His creatures rested together. Wouldn't you have done the same? Don't you love to take time to celebrate together with your children? Well, God did not want a birthday celebration just once a year, but once a week—*every week, on the seventh day,* He wants us to remember that we can rest in His faithfulness. So, He set it apart and made it holy so that His children would have a constant reminder that He is their Creator and eventual Redeemer.

God did not want a birthday celebration just once a year, but once a week—every week, on the seventh day.

By the way, **check this out!** We start to get a glimpse of the creation-redemption theme running from Genesis to Revelation when we analyze this **one** word in Genesis 2:2: "completed" (as it relates to the seventh-day rest celebrating the completion of Creation). The word used in the Septuagint (LXX, the Greek translation of the Old Testament) for "completed" in Genesis 2:2 is the same Greek root word that Jesus cried out at the cross!! "It is **completed!**" "It is **finished!**" "It has been **accomplished!**" (John 19:30). Woo-hoo! OK, OK, I am getting ahead of myself.

I am here! Hang on!

Many newspapers, magazines, TV shows, and newscasts told her story. Even today, it is called a miracle. This is how Genelle Guzman-McMillan, the last survivor to be rescued from the horrific 9/11 Twin Towers terrorist attack, told her story to the *New York Post:*

I Will Give You *Rest*

I was on the 64th floor of the North Tower when the plane hit. There wasn't any smoke at first and no fire. My co-workers were calling the Port Authority, who we worked for, and they were telling us, "Stay there, we'll send someone to get you."

We turned on the TV, and that's when we learned it was a terrorist attack. We waited about an hour and then headed for the stairwell, and I went out in front with my friend Rosa.

At the 13th floor I bent over to take off my shoe, and the entire wall caved on top of me. I could feel chunks of the building hitting me. Then the whole staircase tipped and came down, but the way it fell, it curled over me, and I was in kind of a little pocket.

My feet were pinned, my head was squashed between two pieces of concrete. I could only move my left hand.

When I opened my eyes, I thought I'd gone blind. It scared me so much to have my eyes open and be in the pitch black. I heard a man crying. "Help, help, help," he said. I shouted back, "Hello?"

But I never heard his voice again. I just lay there, and prayed for someone to find me. I had no idea how much time passed. I'd felt around with my left hand and there was a small opening near my head. I put my hand through and prayed.

"Please, God, I can't take the pain."

I kept praying for I don't know how long, and then someone grabbed my hand. "I'm Paul," he said to me. "I'm here. Hang on. The rescuers are coming." It took a long time for them to find me, but he kept holding my hand, keeping me calm. "Just stay with me," he'd say.

They cut me free after 27 hours of being trapped in the rubble, I later learned.

My right leg was crushed, and my head had swelled up, but otherwise I was fine. When my boyfriend got to me at the hospital, the first thing I said was, "Write down the name Paul so I don't forget."

I never found him though. Nobody could tell me who he was. It's a mystery to me where he came from. I would love to meet him. Whoever he was, he was an angel.[2]

And even though this story was spread widely through media, no one ever found Paul. The rescuers said they could see no one holding her hand when they found her and that no one in their team had that name. And yet that hand and that voice kept her alive: "I'm here. Hang on. The rescuers are coming." It was all she had, and it kept her calm.

Back in Genesis 3, the beautiful world God had created for His children collapsed when they sinned. Eventually expelled from Paradise, the first couple saw the walls of their perfect immortal future come tumbling down, and they were buried under an impenetrable pile of rubble, becoming mortals and utterly helpless. A spirit of unrest crept into their souls: fear, shame, and blame dominated their thoughts and feelings (Genesis 3:7–12). But God's voice was heard,

> The beautiful world God had created for His children collapsed when they sinned.

and His hand extended to the human race as He uttered, for the very first time, the words of His covenant that He made with us when we became handicapped by sin. Genesis 3:15 is a most passionate statement by God that this is not the end for the human race. No! The powerful hand of God was extended to rescue them, and His voice was heard loud and clear: "I AM HERE! Hang on! A RESCUER is coming!"

The Rescuer: Closest of kin

One of the most intriguing themes running through Scripture is the one commonly referred to as the "kinsman-redeemer." For the nation of Israel, when someone came to be in distress and was in need of being rescued, their closest relative could legally step in. If a man could no longer support himself, he could give up his property or inheritance; and if that wasn't enough, he could turn himself into a slave to pay his debt. What a terrible situation! But wait! There was a light at the end of the tunnel! The nearest kinsman, the closest relative, could act on his behalf: he could purchase the property or land and restore it to its original owner or pay the ransom for the enslaved relative to be set free. The *closest of kin* claimed responsibility for the relative in distress. Can you imagine being so destitute and so lost, and then you hear the news about your kinsman-redeemer on his way to rescue you? Woohoo! A person buried under an impenetrable rubble of slavery or financial destitution could REST in the understanding that a RESCUER was on the way!

The word in Hebrew for the kinsman-redeemer is *go'el*. The *go'el* had many roles regarding the destitute relative. Leviticus 25 is one of many chapters to explain in detail some of the laws of redemption. We see this in the following examples:

1. *To redeem property that was given up by a poor relative.* "If a fellow countryman of yours becomes so poor he has to sell part of his property, then his nearest kinsman [*go'el*] is to come and buy back what his relative has sold" (Leviticus 25:25). For further information, please see verses 26–34.

2. To redeem a relative who had sold himself into slavery. "Now if . . . a countryman of yours becomes so poor with regard to him as to sell himself to a stranger who is sojourning with you, or to the descendants of a stranger's family, then he shall have redemption right after he has been sold. One of his brothers may redeem him . . . or one of his blood relatives from his family may redeem him" (Leviticus 25:47–49). For further study, see verses 50–54.

3. To avenge the blood of a murdered relative. The *go'el haddam* was the "avenger of blood." The guilty party could rest in a city of refuge (see Numbers 35:12, 19–27; Deuteronomy 19:6, 12; Joshua 20:2).

4. To appear in a lawsuit as a helper for a relative. The *go'el* would make sure that justice was done (see Proverbs 23:11; Jeremiah 50:34; Psalm 119:154).

5. The go'el was the one who would marry the widow of a close relative who had died without descendants. This was in order to provide for the widow and to ensure that the family lineage would continue, thus removing shame from the kin (Deuteronomy 25:5, 6; the whole book of Ruth is written around this concept).

Can you imagine a person in slavery, destitute, without property, or in a lawsuit? Can you imagine the helplessness and the hopelessness he experienced? But can you visualize the happiness and relief that the person started to feel when he saw his *go'el*? The *go'el* was the redeemer, the one who looked after your safety and did whatever was necessary to take your shame away and bring you back to freedom. Your closest of kin was your hope and safety.

If a person had no *go'el* and lost everything, he or she still had hope and could rest assured that Yahweh, the Lord Himself, would extend a rescuing hand. And He had set reminders of this incredible reality through REST celebra-

Your closest of kin was your hope and safety.

tions on the seventh day of the week, festivities on the seventh month, the sabbatical seventh year, and finally the year of jubilee (seven times seven years). God Himself would be their ultimate *Go'el,* who would step in on the year of jubilee. Every seven times seven years, God would step in for everyone:

> You are also to count off seven sabbaths of years for yourself, seven times seven years, so that you have the time of the seven sabbaths of years, namely, forty-nine years. You shall then sound a ram's horn abroad on the tenth day of the seventh month; on the day of atonement you shall sound a horn all through your land. You shall thus

consecrate the fiftieth year and proclaim a release [or liberty] through the land to all its inhabitants. It shall be a jubilee for you, and each of you shall return to his own property, and each of you shall return to his family (Leviticus 25:8–10).

In the seventh year and in the year of jubilee, Yahweh Himself, by His own legal right, would step in and become the Kinsman-Redeemer, fulfilling different roles of the *Go'el.* Everyone became free. The concepts of the Sabbath day, Sabbath year, the Day of Atonement, and the year of jubilee would be forever linked with redemption.

It is very interesting to me that the Liberty Bell, the symbol of freedom in the United States of America, has this very verse inscribed on it: *Lev. XXV:X. Proclaim LIBERTY throughout all the land unto all the inhabitants thereof.* That is where the bell gets its name.

I want to share a little detail with you that I think is amazing! In the Greek Old Testament, the Day of Atonement was called "the Sabbath of Sabbaths, a rest" (*sabbata sabbaton, anapausis*) (Leviticus 16:31). The people of Israel could have a complete *sabbatical rest* for their souls because their sins were atoned for through the blood of an animal that pointed to the ultimate sacrifice of Jesus on the cross. The word *anapausis* used for *rest* in Leviticus

16:31 in the Septuagint is very important for our study, because it is the same word used by Jesus in His invitation: "Come to Me . . . I will give you rest [*anapausō*]. . . . YOU WILL FIND REST [*anapausis*] FOR YOUR SOULS" (Matthew 11:28, 29).

We will analyze this word in detail in chapter 4. But until then, let me tell you that I am SO amazed that God set so many "rest celebrations" so that human beings would remember that He wasn't about to leave them in the wheat

He committed Himself to become our Rescuer.

fields or under the rubble! NO!! He wanted His children to trust Him, to live without anxiety, and to have a "rested soul" because HE would provide **rescue!**

Our *Go'el*

And this is where it gets really good! The next sentence is the most important one to understand in this whole book, so read it twice if necessary.

When God created us in His image, He pledged Himself to carry out a rescue plan, because He was our "Closest of Kin." He is our *Go'el*. He committed Himself to become our Rescuer. From the very beginning, the concepts of creation and redemption were linked together. When my mother had a child in her image, she pledged herself to rescue me when necessary. She was my rescuer. My mother would not have even entertained the thought of leaving me in the middle of the fields, just because I had become handicapped! No! She was my **mother!** And my rescuer. God is our Father and Redeemer (*Go'el*), and He wouldn't do that either:

> You, O LORD, are our Father,
> Our Redeemer [*Go'el*] from of old is Your name
>   (Isaiah 63:16).

Go'el is used in the Scriptures as a descriptive name for God, usually translated as *Redeemer* in our English Bibles. It highlights His mighty acts of redemption on behalf of His people (Exodus 6:6; 15:13). Especially in the book of Isaiah, God constantly reminds us that He is our Kinsman-Redeemer, our *Go'el*. I am particularly touched when He reminds us to "fear not" because He has done His job as our *Go'el:*

> But now, thus says the LORD, your Creator, O Jacob,
> And He who formed you, O Israel,
> "Do not fear, for I have redeemed [*Go'el-ed*] you;
> I have called you by name; you are Mine!"
>   (Isaiah 43:1).

Jesus would be the One to become flesh, become our Brother, and redeem us without money (see Isaiah 52:3). He redeemed us with His blood; He came to die. That was the purpose: to pay the ransom because He is our *Go'el*.

Jesus Himself stated that this was the purpose of His death, and in His explanation we find a word usually associated with the *go'el* and the payment that was offered for the enslaved relative: "For even the Son of Man did not come to be served, but to serve, and to give His life a *ransom* for many" (Mark 10:45; emphasis added). Jesus redeemed us, He will redeem our land (the new earth will be right here, we'll be back to where we started in Genesis 1! [see Revelation 22]), and He will produce an offspring from a race that was dead (see Isaiah 53:10)! Furthermore, He appears in court in our place and will avenge our blood at the end of time! Jesus fulfills all the roles of the *Go'el*. Praise God for our Kinsman-Redeemer!

Resting in His faithfulness

The whole Bible is the story of how God rescued His children and why we can go through life without anxiety, *resting* in His ability to save us. You see, when humankind chose to sin, they became mortals (Romans 5:12–21). They were handicapped. They could not save themselves. They were dying, because "the wages of sin is death" (Romans 6:23)! The evil forces never expected that love would win! The devil thought that we were forever buried under an impenetrable pile of rubble. Perhaps even humans themselves thought that they were beyond redemption!

But "where sin increased, grace abounded all the more" (Romans 5:20). Our *Go'el* stepped in and stretched out His powerful hand to save us. He left us constant and ongoing "celebrations of rest" that we may never forget His commitment to His creation and beloved children: "I AM HERE. HANG ON! YOU WILL BE RESCUED!"

In other words: **rest in the faithfulness of Jesus,** that He will do what He said He would do! So take a deep breath and **relax.** We know how it ends; and the **rescue** is more than successful through the blood of the Lamb.

Rest in the faithfulness of Jesus, that He will do what He said He would do!

Perhaps you are already starting to experience what He promised. Fill in the blank space with your name: "_____: Come to Me. . . . **You will find rest for your soul**" (Matthew 11:28, 29; author's paraphrase).

Rest in Jesus' Faithfulness!!

1. Sections of this chapter are taken from "The Rescuer," in *Surprised by Love* (Nampa, ID: Pacific Press® Publishing Association, 2010).

2. Ginger Adams Otis, "Miracle Tale From the Towers: Genelle Guzman-McMillan," *The New York Post,* September 11, 2011, http://nypost.com/2011/09/11/miracle-tale-from-the-towers-genelle-guzman-mcmillan/.

CHAPTER 3

REST in Jesus' PROVISION!!

Even though I have been passionate about God since my childhood, it took actual pain to bring about my real spiritual awakening. It was in the darkness of the soul that my understanding of God traveled all the way from my head to my heart, and I learned to fully trust in Him both for my salvation as well as for my daily life. During this time, the concept of **soul rest** became a lifesaver for me, because I had realized that I was no longer in control of my own life. The truth is that I was never really in control even though I thought I was. HE WAS and IS in control! And this is something that I need to remember every morning!

At that time, several years ago, I started reading books on the concept of having a *"sabbathed soul"* and a *"sabbathed life."* The word *sabbath* comes from the Hebrew verb *sabat,* which means "to rest" (Genesis 2:2). The possibility of living my life free of anxiety seemed more than attractive. All my life I had lived with a plan B for everything, always having a contingency strategy in place, and then a plan C if B should fail. Sometimes I found myself going through plans all the way from A to Z, but still, it wasn't working. So I decided to turn the wheel over to God, because I couldn't carry the weight of the world on my shoulders anymore. I am sure that God whispered a sigh of relief: "FINALLY!"

The possibility of living my life free of anxiety seemed more than attractive.

One morning I shared my newfound **soul-rest** concept with my husband and made an important declaration to back it up because I wanted the whole world to know about it. I told him, "I have decided what I want to have written on my TOMBSTONE when I die."

If he was surprised, he didn't show it: "Really! What is it?"

"I want it to say these exact words: 'SHE WAS A SABBATHED SOUL. SHE ENTERED **GOD'S REST** LONG BEFORE SHE DIED.' " I still want to be known like that. I think it reveals what I've found in Jesus.

Now, to understand the rest of the story, you must know that my husband, Patrick, has a great and unusual sense of humor, and many times he says and does the unexpected. But even so, I don't think you can imagine the look on my face when ten minutes later, my husband calls me from a tombstone engraving shop. "Would you like those words engraved on marble or metal?"

I admit that I was speechless. You see, I usually have a lot to say about a lot of things, but this time I was totally dumbstruck! When no words came out of my mouth, he started laughing. He had gone to an engraving shop to pick up a little trophy he had ordered for his granddaughter and noticed that they also engraved tombstones and decided to play a practical joke on me—very successfully, I must say!

The truth is that if we are to live in real peace, we all need to surrender to God's will; we desperately need to live with *sabbathed souls,* **resting** in our Father's ability to provide and guide according to His will, which is always the best way! No anxiety; just experiencing *rest* in the core of our souls. God wants us to enjoy life to the fullest, even during difficult seasons! He desires us to become like children, living in awe of His grace, even though we might not have all the answers for everything!

The truth is that if we are to live in real peace, we all need to surrender to God's will.

I was touched by a blessing offered in the ordination of the Christian author Brennan Manning:

May all of your expectations be frustrated,

May all of your plans be thwarted,
May all of your desires be withered into nothingness,
That you may experience the powerlessness and
    poverty of a child,
And can sing and dance in the love of God the
    Father, Son and Holy Spirit.[1]

Yes! At some point we need to let go and let God! I was a very hard nut to crack. But God found a way, and now I have become a "wounded healer with a *sabbathed soul*." I don't have all the answers (not by a long shot!), but my heavenly Daddy does. And just as a child I could rest in the backseat of the car because my daddy was driving and knew where we were going, so I can rest now for the same reason! Let's get started. Another deep breath, and here we go!

A *restful* assurance

As we studied in chapter 1, the biblical stories and characters within God's covenant all point to the redemption that God would accomplish through Jesus on behalf of His creation. In the first chapter, we discussed the Passover lamb in Egypt, chronicled in Exodus 12, and how it served as a remarkable metaphor to help us understand that Jesus would die for us as the "Pass-over" Lamb (1 Corinthians 5:7).

However, that was not the only pointer to the

redemptive work of Jesus by far. The Bible is replete with reminders about God's salvation. God uttered the covenant of redemption right after the Fall in the presence of Adam and Eve (Genesis 3:15), and He repeated and developed the same covenant with Noah (Genesis 9; you will find the *rainbow* there!). Then we get to Abram in Genesis 12 (God would eventually give Abram a new name: Abraham). God gives him a striking promise of **hope**: "In you all the families of the earth will be blessed" (Genesis 12:3).

This prophecy pointed to the reality of being set right with God through faith in the righteousness of Jesus, who was Abraham's descendant (Galatians 3:8). Even though Abram was childless, God promised him descendants as countless as the stars (Genesis 15:5), and this is where we get the first clear statement of "righteousness by faith" in the Bible: "And he [Abram] believed in the LORD, and He accounted it to him for righteousness" (verse 6, NKJV). There was *hope* because God gave the *assurance*! Abram was made right with God because he believed in what God was promising (even though he didn't have any "proof" to see it). That's how Abraham became known for his faith (Romans 4:1–4).

I don't know about you, but for me the fact that God is in control of the future makes all the difference in the world! He even told Abram that his offspring would be enslaved and oppressed for four hundred years and then would be delivered (Genesis 15:13, 14)! Abram would die in peace (verse 15), *resting* in the assurance that God had a plan. For years, I carried a large acrylic sign on my key chain to remind me of that fact: "I don't know the Master Plan, but I know the Master who planned it and I am included." Oh, yes! There is *sweet rest* to be found in surrendering ourselves completely to His plan instead of trying to force our plans, because God's plans put our best dreams to shame.

A *restful* provision

Sometimes I wonder how much patience God needs to teach us something "developmentally"! I still remember when I was a little child, and my mom lovingly told me every day that I had to take a nap and rest in the middle of the afternoon! I thought it was such a waste of time! So many places to go and so many games to play! I took a nap because she said so, not because I understood why I needed it. Now I wish I could take a nap every day! I still need to make sure I get enough rest every night to be effective and productive the following day!

God lovingly taught His people to *rest* in Him. And He did it gradually and developmentally, as they grew in their knowledge of Him. God *rested* in His completion of Creation (Genesis 2:2), now His children had to learn to *rest* in His ability to redeem and to re-create them. So as time went by, God kept adding more and more meaning to the *Sabbath rest,* until we finally understand its full significance at the cross. Let's look at our original diagram again, now in regards to the *sabbatical rest* God wanted us to experience in our souls:

For the purpose of our study, I have drawn only five

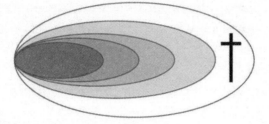

expansions of the understanding of God's *rest,* even though there are many more, until we get to the full understanding of our *rest in the salvific work of Jesus on our behalf.*

Let's imagine that the first and darkest circle in the diagram represents God *resting* on the seventh day, celebrating the completion

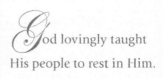

God lovingly taught His people to rest in Him.

of Creation (Genesis 2:2). Now, as we get to the time of Moses and the nation of Israel, how could God teach them that they could *rest* in His ability to provide for them? As usual, I am **so glad** you asked! The first time that the seventh day is actually called "Sabbath" in the Bible, offering an expanded understanding of the Sabbath as a "day of rest," is found in Exodus 16, in the narrative about manna. It provides a subsequent step after the first use of the verb *sabat* in Genesis 2:2, where God *rested* after the work of creation. These people had been oppressed for hundreds of years, as God had foretold to Abraham (Genesis 15:13, 14). Now they needed to *trust* the God of heaven and earth to **provide** for their every need, including their daily bread!

And God reminded them through the *Sabbath rest* that He is the ultimate Provider:

> Then he [Moses] said to them, "This is what the LORD meant: Tomorrow is a sabbath observance, a holy sabbath [*sabbata anapausis,* LXX] to the LORD. Bake what you will bake and boil what you will boil, and all that is left over put aside to be kept until morning." . . .
>
> ". . . See, the LORD has given you the sabbath; therefore He gives you bread for two days on the sixth day. Remain every man in his place; let no man go out of his place on the seventh day." So the people rested [*esabbatisen*] on the seventh day (Exodus 16:23, 29, 30).

Rest in Jesus' Provision!!

God was their **Provider**! This experience is represented by the second circle in our diagram. It is a new and expanded understanding of *Sabbath rest*. God would miraculously preserve the heavenly bread (take a moment to read Exodus 16, which is a phenomenal narrative!) every week, so that they could *rest* in His ability to provide for them! Woo-hoo! If we could all come to that understanding, how *restful* our lives would be! But we forget so easily; no wonder God created a weekly reminder for our forgetful hearts! But wait! We just got started!

> *One of the main reasons why we get anxious and fearful is because we forget who we are and to whom we belong!*

A *restful* identity

One of the main reasons why we get anxious and fearful is because we forget who we are and to whom we belong! I love the fact that God constantly reminds us to "FEAR NOT!" (Some scholars have counted 365 such reminders in the Bible! One per each day of the year!) I guess, if we had been slaves for four hundred years, it would have taken a toll on our self-worth as well and on remembering *who and whose we are,* just as it happens when someone has been abused, violated, or has gone through a traumatic experience in some other way. The people of Israel needed to be reminded that the One who had taken them out of Egypt and had acted miraculously on their behalf was none other than the **Creator** of heaven and earth! So, that's the third circle in our diagram. Aside from remembering that Yahweh is their **Provider,** they also need to be reminded to *rest,* knowing that they are children of the **Creator!**

God considered this so important that He brought to their attention a weekly feast of remembrance as part of the Ten Commandments so that they would not forget who they were and to whom they belonged!

"I am the LORD [Yahweh] your God, who brought you out of the land of Egypt, out of the house of slavery. . . .

"Remember the *sabbath* day, to keep it holy. Six days you shall labor and do all your work, but the seventh day is a *sabbath* of the LORD [Yahweh] your God, in it you shall not do any work. . . . For in six days the LORD made the heavens and the earth, the sea and all that is in them, and *rested* on the seventh day; therefore the LORD blessed the sabbath day and made it holy" (Exodus 20:2, 8–11, emphasis added).

Rest in Jesus' Provision!!

How important it was to be reminded that they were to *rest* just like God *rested*. They were His! Oh, what a different world this would be if we all remembered *whose* we are, and celebrated that on a weekly basis! "See how great a love the Father has bestowed on us, that we would be called children of God; and such we are" (1 John 3:1). I am amazed at how God begins expanding the meaning of *rest* in Him! And we are just getting started! We are only in the second book of the Bible! Don't worry, we won't analyze all the books of the Bible, but we do need to go over at least two more expanded circles of the meaning of *rest* in the diagram. It is SO important to remember that **everything**, including our *weekly rest,* ultimately relates to the Creator-Redeemer, who is **victorious** on our behalf. That's why we *rest*! That's why we can't stop our developmental exploration until we get to the cross!

A *restful* freedom

You would think that everyone who is set **free** starts living as a **free** person. But this is not so; and we see it all around us daily. Perhaps you have heard stories about soldiers who, for decades after a war, had not realized that the war was over. The following is one such amazing story, as told in an online world news article, titled "Japanese WWII Soldier Who Refused to Surrender for 29 Years Dies."

I Will Give You *Rest*

A Japanese soldier who hid in the jungle and refused to surrender until 29 years after the end of World War II died on Friday [January 17, 2014], aged 91.

Hiroo Onada was one of the last of many so-called "hold-outs" dotted around Asia who refused to give themselves up after Japanese Emperor Hirohito surrendered to the Allies in 1945. . . .

The soldier became a war hero in Japan after he hid on the Philippine island of Lubang until March 1974. He only gave himself up after his former commander flew out and reversed his orders from 1945, which had instructed him to spy on U.S. troops. . . .

Japan had several dozen other men who stayed in various parts of Asia long after the war. Another hold-out, Sgt. Shoichi Yokoi, emerged from the jungle in 1972 to widespread praise in Japan.[2]

Can you imagine hiding and surviving in the jungle for thirty years after the war was over? How about us? Are we living with the joy of salvation that Jesus achieved for us, or are we still under the yoke of fear, slavery, and oppression in our souls? Well, Israel needed yet another insight in their understanding of why they should hold a

Rest in Jesus' Provision!!

weekly feast of rest, and it came to them in the second reading of the law—in the book of Deuteronomy.

The Ten Commandments are repeated to them again, and this time their understanding of the *reason* for their weekly rest was expanded:

Are we living with the joy of salvation that Jesus achieved for us, or are we still under the yoke of fear, slavery, and oppression in our souls?

" 'I am the LORD [Yahweh] your God who brought you out of the land of Egypt, out of the house of slavery. . . .

" 'Observe the *sabbath* day to keep it holy, as the LORD your God commanded you. Six days you shall labor and do all your work, but the seventh day is a *sabbath* of the LORD your God. . . . You shall *remember* that you were a slave in the land of Egypt, and the LORD your God brought you out of there by a mighty hand and by an outstretched arm; therefore the LORD your God commanded you to observe the Sabbath day' " (Deuteronomy 5:6, 12–15; emphasis added).

Did you get that? **Freedom** and **redemption** were

added to the ever-expanding understanding of the *Sabbath rest*. This weekly "feast of remembrance" not only reminded them that God, who created the heavens and the earth, was their Provider and their Creator and that they were His, but it also was to remind them that they were no longer slaves! They were **free**! They had been **redeemed** from slavery! Woo-hoo! Yes!

There are two radically different types of Christians today: **enslaved** and **redeemed**!! And you can usually tell the difference by walking into a church or meeting somebody personally! It is sad to see so many Christians still hiding in the "religious jungle," just barely surviving, after Jesus' loud cry was heard throughout the universe, more than two thousand years ago: "IT IS FINISHED!" (John 19:30). Yes! God made sure we know: "If the Son sets you FREE, you shall be **free indeed**!" (John 8:36; emphasis added).

A *restful* completion

In the Old Testament, there are many other such expansions of the meaning of *rest* pointing to the ultimate reality in Jesus; for example, the *rest* that God promised to the Davidic kings, who also were representatives of Israel. God would give them *rest* from their enemies, and they would dwell in peace. Two of these instances are found in 2 Samuel 7:11 and 1 Chronicles

22:9; these are of particular importance to us because the Greek Old Testament utilizes the exact word and verbal tense used by Jesus in His invitation: "Come . . . and I will give you *rest*" (Matthew 11:28; emphasis added). We will devote the entire next chapter to Jesus' offer and promise of rest in Matthew 11:28–30.

As we get to the prophets, the concept of *rest* is expanded to the ultimate reality in Jesus: the Messianic age, which we call eternal life. A life with no pain, no hunger, no evil, no broken relationships, no wounds—just *complete rest*. This complete rest will be brought by Jesus, the promised descendant of David, who will break the yoke of oppression: "For thus says the LORD GOD, 'Behold, I Myself will search for My sheep and seek them out. . . . I will feed My flock and I will lead them to *rest*.' . . . 'Then I will set over them one shepherd, My servant David, and he will feed them; he will feed them himself and be their shepherd' " (Ezekiel 34:11, 15, 23; emphasis added). We will also discuss this topic further in the next chapter.

Perhaps one of the saddest things for me is to see people who keep a "sabbatical rest" without having discovered God's *real rest* and its true meaning, thus, in many ways still remaining enslaved, without the ability to celebrate their redemption. That's why the fifth circle expansion of our diagram will focus on the ultimate restful reality accomplished by Jesus on our behalf, even though there are many more developmental expansions to the meaning of *Sabbath rest* in the Old and New Testaments.

The author of Hebrews utters the sad news that many of the people of God never fully entered or comprehended the ultimate meaning of the *sabbatical rest*. They never came to fully believe that just as God had *completed* creation, so Jesus *completed* the work needed for our redemption. In some Bibles, Hebrews 4 is introduced with a significant title, such as the one found in the *New American Standard Bible:* "The Believer's Rest." And this is what two of the most important verses on this topic explain: "So there remains a *Sabbath rest* for the people of God. For the one who has entered *His rest* has himself also *rested* from his works, *as* God did from His" (Hebrews 4:9, 10; emphasis added). There you go! That's the ultimate meaning! And guess what? It is found at the cross!

> *Many of the people of God never fully entered or comprehended the ultimate meaning of the sabbatical rest.*

A *sabbathed* soul

Have you ever had the amazing experience of having

a baby fall asleep in your arms? I will never forget when my step-granddaughter was a little baby. One afternoon she wouldn't go to sleep, so I took her in my arms and started singing and softly patting her tiny back. All of a sudden she fell fast asleep, and I could feel her whole weight on my arm! She didn't know that she was suspended quite a distance from the floor; she didn't even know I was standing. But she had let go completely and now was fully *resting* in my arms. And at that moment, I started a conversation with God that I will never forget! I asked God, "Is this what You meant when You said that You wanted us to trust You and to live with complete *rest*? Is this how You meant that our whole being would *rest* in Your arms, because we surrender completely to You?" At that sacred moment, I had a very real visualization of what a *sabbathed soul* looks and feels like!

And so it is in the Bible, where the topic of *rest* is developed, that we discover that God wants us to enter His *rest* before we die. He wants

I don't have to wait till my tombstone is engraved in order to fully *rest* in Christ

us to have a *sabbathed soul*, to live in *perfect rest*, because He is our Provider, Creator, Redeemer, and has been faithful to accomplish everything that was necessary for our salvation. I don't have to wait till my tombstone is engraved in order to fully *rest* in Christ. I can start today. You can start TODAY!

Let's make sure we really get it! Let's make sure we take Him at His word! Fill in your name in the blank space:

For _____, who has entered His rest has himself/ herself also rested from his/her works, as God did from His. (Hebrews 4:10; author's paraphrase).

Feel lighter? I sure do! Woo-hoo!

---

1. "Century Marks," *Christian Century,* April 16, 2014, 9.
2. Arata Yamamoto and Alexander Smith, "Japanese WWII Soldier Who Refused to Surrender for 29 Years Dies," NBC News, January 17, 2014, http://worldnews.nbcnews.com /_news/2014/01/17/22336496-japanese-wwii-soldier-who-refused -to-surrender-for-29-years-dies?lite.

Chapter 4

REST in Jesus' PROMISE!!

Some time ago, I posted a picture on my Facebook time line. That's when I realized how "soul-tired" most of the people in my generation really are! It was a photo of an overworked and exhausted young woman who had fallen asleep at her desk, in the midst of piles of unfinished paperwork and sticky notes with deadlines on them. Very soon I started receiving many comments from people who seemed to relate perfectly with this weary person. The caption under the picture was encouraging everyone who was *heavy-laden* to come to Jesus to receive *real rest* (see Matthew 11:28–30).

One of the comments was from a radio broadcaster (thanks, Chuck!) who suggested that I start recording short, one-minute messages for radio and podcasts that would encourage people with thoughts like this caption under the picture. This is how our minute-long daily devotional program *Plug Into Life* was born. You can find it on our Jesus 101 app, iTunes podcasts, or at our

I Will Give You *Rest*

Jesus101.tv Web site as well as through many other venues. It is a sixty-second devotional "for busy people on the go."

Within three months, we had tens of thousands of people listening daily to these one-minute messages of encouragement. The truth is that we all need encouragement. We all are desperate to see the light at the end of the tunnel. We all seem to have endless responsibilities, deadlines, and trials that make us so exhausted that we barely have time to pause long enough to hear Jesus' offer of rest.

Jesus' invitation, "Come . . . all who are weary and heavy-laden, and I will give you rest" (Matthew 11:28), is as relevant today as when Matthew wrote it down in the first century of the Christian era. Jesus' offer is so **real** that it seems to be written just for me, and I am sure that you get the same impression. And the truth is that this "weariness" is not just physical but spiritual and emotional as well. We all yearn for a sense of wholeness and of spiritual refreshment and restoration. We are all longing for a Woo-hoo moment when we find wholeness! We want the joy of our salvation to be restored in the core of our souls; maybe that's

We all yearn for a sense of wholeness and of spiritual refreshment and restoration.

why Jesus said, "And YOU WILL FIND *REST FOR YOUR SOULS*" (verse 29; emphasis added). Our hearts are worn out in the struggles of life; Jesus knows about this and offers us a remedy. In this chapter, we will examine Jesus' offer to give *rest* to our weary souls, which we all need so badly.

Come all! I will give you *rest*

For many years, I have been intrigued by the apparently deliberate juxtaposition found in Matthew 11:25–12:14. First, Jesus offers His own *rest* (the Greek word is *anapausis*) in Matthew 11:28–30 and then proclaims Himself the Lord of the *Sabbath* in the next narrative (Greek *sabbaton,* see Matthew 12:8). Take a moment to read these seventeen verses (Matthew 11:28–12:14). When we realize that the material found in Matthew 11:28–30 is unique to Matthew, this juxtaposition becomes increasingly intriguing. Jesus' offer of *rest* immediately precedes the only two episodes in this Gospel that occur on the *Sabbath*.

I know that our modern thought process creates a mental visualization of overworked people coming to Jesus for some peace and quiet: "Come to Me, all of you who are weary and heavy-laden, and I will give you *rest*. . . . You will find *rest* for your souls" (Matthew 11:28, 29; author's paraphrase). And this is certainly something we all need. But there is so much more.

I Will Give You *Rest*

For example, most people miss the link between these verses and the *Sabbath rest* concept as well as the two *Sabbath* stories that follow this promise of *rest*. So we must start pondering some pertinent questions: What is Matthew trying to convey with the intercalation of these *rest* verses at this stage of the Gospel? What is this *rest* that Jesus offers (Matthew 11:28, 29)? What does Jesus mean when He says, "I will give you *rest*" and "YOU WILL FIND *REST*" (verses 28, 29; emphasis added)? Why did Matthew position Jesus' promise of *rest* right before these two Sabbath stories? These and other similar questions led me to do an in-depth study of these few verses, which I continued for a period of eight years. I began the work on my PhD dissertation with these simple questions in mind; but the results of my research, which taught me to interpret these verses in the light of the identity and mission of Jesus Christ, totally reshaped my understanding of the *sabbath rest* and in turn changed my life and ministry forever.[1]

So, let's get started. I believe you will find it very interesting that the term *sabbath* is used eleven times in Matthew's Gospel, and eight of these occurrences appear in the two consecutive passages (Matthew 12:1–8; 9–14) that follow Jesus' double promise of *rest* (Matthew 11:28, 29). The conglomeration of the term *sabbath* in this section, preceded by Jesus' offer of *rest*, cannot be a coincidence. And I know that you will get really excited when you read some of the findings that I am about to share with you!

Rest means *what?*

One evening we had a great time at a friend's house. He has a lovely family, and I have known him since his youth. He was telling me that since his children had started asking him questions about his religious beliefs he himself had learned a lot about God. He had found out that he did not really have all the answers that he thought he had. I think most of us have realized this fact at some point in our lives. Sometimes as adults we are more afraid to ask questions about our own religious beliefs than children are. Perhaps we feel threatened by the prospect of going deeper because we are afraid that by taking a closer look at even one of our foundational beliefs our whole religious structure might collapse like the walls of Jericho.

Having pondered these verses for many years, I finally started digging deep. The first question I had to ask was, What was the usage of the word *rest* (*anapausis*) in the Greek translation of the Old Testament (called Septuagint or LXX), which was used by the New Testament writers? What did Matthew's audience understand when they heard the promise of *rest* in light of their Greek translation of the Jewish Scriptures? Was this word *anapausis* related to the Sabbath in any way? Wait till you hear the answer! You may want to sit down!

There are 137 occurrences of this root word *rest* (*anapausis*) in the Septuagint, and I studied each one of them in detail. Of these occurrences, twenty-four are found in the Law (Pentateuch), nineteen in the historical books, forty-four in the poetic books, and fifty in the prophetic books.[2]

> One of the things they heard loud and clear was: "Come to Me, all you who are weary and heavy-laden, and I will give you the *real sabbatical rest.*"

And check this out! In the Law, the first five books of the Bible, the term predominantly relates to a *sabbatical rest to the Lord* (whether on the seventh day, on the holy convocations of the seventh month, or on the seventh year). Furthermore, *sabbatical rest* is the exclusive meaning of the term in Exodus and Leviticus, where the word is used only for this purpose. Did you get that? In the Law, the Greek word chosen by Jesus in Matthew means *sabbatical rest*! Therefore, Matthew's audience had a much deeper understanding of Jesus' offer of rest, and their mental visualization of the word was much more than a hammock under a palm tree where they could take a nap. Oh, no, no, no! One of the things they heard loud and clear was: "Come to Me, all you who are weary and heavy-laden, and I will give you the *real sabbatical rest*. . . . You will find the *real sabbatical rest for your souls*" (Matthew 11:28, 29; author's paraphrase). Woo-hoo! Now we are getting somewhere! But wait, there is more, much more . . .

Rest also means *this*!

And it keeps getting more and more exciting! Let me try to share a bit more. I think it will be helpful, besides I get super WOO-HOO excited about it!

In the *historical and prophetic* books of the Septuagint, the most prominent meaning of the word *rest* (*anapausis*) is the promise of a "peaceful dwelling" for the people of God. This *rest* was promised to Israel through David and Solomon (2 Samuel 7:11; 1 Chronicles 22:9) and through the future Davidic ruler (Jesus) who was to come (e.g., Ezekiel 34:15, 23, 24). Josephus attests that in Matthew's time, the word *anapausis* had become normative for "sabbath day of rest."[3] They believed their weekly *anapausis* was pointing to the Messianic age, which we call eternal life and/or heaven. Their weekly Sabbath on the seventh day was a celebratory "appetizer" of heaven. WOW! I love it!

When Jesus offers "*rest* for your souls" to all those who are weary and burdened, He is actually saying that those who heed His invitation now enter into the Sabbath rest in its fullest sense because they *rest in Him*. Thus, they find the full meaning of the weekly *Sabbath rest celebration* in the identity and mission of Jesus. Furthermore, they would start experiencing the "age to come" already, in their souls, because Jesus is the one who offers and guarantees the eternal age of rest. I can't even begin to tell you what an incredible joy this understanding has brought into my own walk with Jesus Christ. He is **my complete rest!** And I commemorate my redemption in Him every week! So in the time of Jesus, everyone must have been celebrating the fact that they had finally found the true meaning of the *Sabbath rest* in Him, right? Not really.

But wait a minute!

I have heard a story (I don't know its source; if you do, please let me know) about a little girl who wondered why her mother always engaged in what seemed to her to be a strange routine. After preparing the family's special recipe, which was a delicious fruit tart, she observed that her mom would cut off and throw away a large chunk, then place the remaining tart to be baked in the oven. So one day the little girl asked her mom, "Why do you always cut off and throw away part of the tart?" Her mother paused for a moment and then responded pensively, "Honey, I don't really know. Your grandma always did that, so that's the way I learned to do it. But why don't we go visit Grandma and ask her?"

So both mother and daughter arrived at the grandmother's house with a rather high level of curiosity. This time it was the mother who took the initiative and asked the question: "Mom, why do you always cut off and throw away a section of the fruit tart?" The answer took both by surprise: "Darling, I have no idea. My mother always did it that way. Why don't we go ask her? Perhaps she can provide an answer." So, the little girl, her mother, and her grandmother all headed to the great-grandma's place. She was happily surprised to see all three coming to visit her at the nursing home. She wondered for a moment if it was her birthday or some other special date that she might have forgotten about, but soon she learned the reason for such an unexpected visit.

This time Grandma spoke up: "All three of us are wondering why our family always throws away a big chunk of that special fruit tart we make before baking it. Can you tell us why we do that?"

"Well, of course! At least I know why I did it! Many years ago, when we had just gotten married, we were quite poor. Someone took pity on us and gifted us a tiny little wood oven that couldn't fit a thing! But I was very eager to bake for my husband and children. I used to make the best fruit tarts in town, but they wouldn't fit in that tiny oven. I had to cut off a section to make them fit so that we could enjoy my savory treats!"

Baffled and a little embarrassed, all three returned home, wondering why in the world they had never asked this question before, and thereby, all these years they had missed a big part of the fruit tart for no reason at all.

Over the years, I have observed some Christians cutting off and throwing away a big chunk of the sweet feast of the *Sabbath rest* that God created for us. Some became so confused as to throw away the whole thing, because it had become dry and bitter. Someone had taught them a routine, perhaps giving them a list of dos and don'ts, and they had always observed the tradition of Sabbath, without knowing the real meaning of *rest* in Christ. But doctrines void of clear gospel understanding and traditions contrary to Christ-centered biblical teaching always leave us dry and rob our souls of the sweet *rest* that God prepared for us through the salvific work of Jesus.

So going back to our text, Matthew's narrative contrasts Jesus' invitation to rest in Matthew 11:28–30 with the Pharisaical perspective on the *Sabbath laws* in Matthew 12:1–14. This contrast is suggestive and deliberate. The adjacency of these two terms in Matthew 11:28–12:14 indicates that there is a strong thematic link. So the time has come to ask the core question: What is the purpose of this *rest-sabbath* juxtaposition? Is Matthew trying to tell us something?

Sabbath versus Jesus?

There are so many things I would like to share with you. There are very significant details in this passage, such as Matthew's use of the word *burden* (*phortion*) in Matthew 11:30. Jesus said, "My *burden* is light." There is only one other place in all of the Gospel of Matthew where the noun "burden" is used, and it relates to the burden of Pharisaic legalism: "They tie up heavy

> *The burden of Jesus is light,* while the burden of the Pharisees is *heavy.*

burdens on men's shoulders" (Matthew 23:4; emphasis added). The burden of Jesus is *light,* while the burden of the Pharisees is *heavy.* This is an intentional juxtaposition, as Matthew records the story of the Pharisees complaining about the disciples doing what is not lawful on the Sabbath right after Jesus' offer of rest (Matthew 12:2). Jesus then challenges them to go back and read their Bibles! Jesus gives examples from the Law and the historical books, and quotes the prophets (verses 1–7) and ends His argument by proclaiming Himself the "Lord of the Sabbath" (verse 8).

Not every Sabbath keeper understood that the Sabbath was a symbol of a full *rest* in Jesus, available only through the salvific work that He accomplished. As a matter of fact, in the Gospels, the most vicious enemies of Jesus were Sabbath keepers. They constantly questioned Jesus, and many rejected Him in the name of the Sabbath.

One such story is narrated in John 9. This has to be one of the most paradoxical stories in all four Gospels! Jesus is rejected in the name of the **Sabbath!** Yes, the Lord of the Sabbath Himself (Matthew 12:8) got rejected because He didn't keep the Sabbath properly! WOW! Can you believe it? What a paradox! Jesus' *rest* was what the Sabbath fully pointed to! How could He possibly breach the Sabbath? Jesus heals a blind man on the Sabbath. The Pharisees hurry to introduce a legal issue: to them Jesus had clearly broken the Sabbath. He heals and does, as well as instructs others to do, things that in their narrow and mistaken understanding are forbidden on Sabbath.

Well, in their own interpretation of the law, that was an offense. The blind man keeps giving his testimony of how he was healed; it's simple and it's powerful. This is his story, and he's sticking to it: "He applied clay to my eyes, and I washed, and I see" (John 9:15). Then the division occurs among the Pharisees. Some focus on the apparent breaking of the Sabbath law, while others concentrate on the magnitude of the "signs" (plural) that Jesus is performing (verse 16). According to their understanding of Sabbath keeping Jesus seems to be a "sinner." After all, the Pharisees are the experts of law keeping. What is going on here? Is their long-accepted interpretation of the Sabbath law being called in for a reexamination?

Unfortunately, this is too much for the religious authorities! The lines are drawn: "You are His disciple, but we are disciples of Moses. We know that God has spoken to

*From the very beginning, the Sabbath was supposed to **point to and celebrate** the work of Jesus in creating and redeeming the human race*

Moses, but as for this man, we do not know where He is from" (verses 28, 29). Then these religious, Sabbath-keeping leaders expel the follower of Jesus from the synagogue. They choose the Sabbath and reject Jesus. They think it is the Sabbath versus Jesus. But it was never meant to be that way. From the very beginning, the Sabbath was supposed to **point to and celebrate** the work of Jesus in creating and redeeming the human race.

Now, let's get back to our verse in Matthew. How could God liberate us from such a schizophrenic and double-minded theology and offer our souls a *true sabbatical rest*? I am SO glad you asked! This is getting exciting! But how do we know we are following the appropriate interpretation of the scriptural Sabbath rest? How do we know who is the God-appointed teacher and leader who takes us to green pastures and quiet waters of rest (see Psalm 23:1–3)?

Kings and shepherds

Over the years, I have collected some information about sheep because they are a commonly used scriptural metaphor to describe the people of God in need of His guidance. In doing so, I have learned that in general sheep are very helpless animals. They can't instinctively find food or water; they need protection from predators; they can easily drown if they try to drink in deep waters; and they can't sleep if there are problems, like tension in the flock or if there are bugs that bother them. Sheep are absolutely and completely dependent on the shepherd to provide everything for them, including a peaceful and quiet place, green pasture, restful waters, and everything else. The sheep don't know where they are or where they are going; they just need to follow their shepherd (they sound just like us, don't they?).

It is so interesting that many biblical authors, including Matthew, write about people and compare them to sheep (e.g., Matthew 9:36; 10:6; 12:11, 12; 15:24; 26:31). This is why I think that this next topic is of the utmost importance for us in order to understand the promise of Jesus: "*I will give you rest*" (Matthew 11:28; emphasis added).

Rest in Jesus' Promise!!

Having grasped the meaning of the noun *"rest"* (*ana-pausis*) in the Septuagint (LXX), it is now pivotal to understand the first saying of Jesus, using the *verb* in the first-person singular and in the future tense. Jesus promises, "I will give rest [*anapausō*]" (Matthew 11:28; in English we use the same word for the verb [verse 28] and the noun [verse 29]). This exact verbal wording, in the first-person singular, appears only three times in the Septuagint (LXX), and all three come from the mouth of the Lord: 2 Samuel 7:11; 1 Chronicles 22:9; and Ezekiel 34:15. The first two occurrences are promises to the Davidic dynasty, and the third relates to the future Davidic king (Jesus).

In 2 Samuel 7, the Lord makes a covenant with David. He reminds David that He took him from following the sheep to be shepherd, leading Israel. After describing a place for Israel without disturbances, the Lord then promises to *give rest* to David: "I will give *rest* [*anapausō*] to you from all your enemies" (2 Samuel 7:11, LXX). The background of 2 Samuel 7:11–14, which contains a direct verbal link to *anapausō*, is of special interest because of Matthew portraying Jesus as the promised Davidic Shepherd King (e.g., Matthew 1:1; 2:6; 9:27; 21:9).

In the second Septuagint occurrence, David is talking to his son Solomon about the promise that the Lord had made to him. Solomon would not only be a man of *rest*, but also the recipient of the same promise the Lord had given to David: "I will give rest [*anapausō*] to him" (1 Chronicles 22:9, LXX). The Lord promised David that He would give him and his son *rest* (rest for the people of Israel through their leaders is implied).

The third and last occurrence of the verb in the first-person singular in the future tense is found in the prophetic books of the Septuagint (Ezekiel 34:15). It follows a prophecy against the shepherds of Israel who were not taking care of the sheep. This next occurrence is the most important among the three to inform the background for the offer of Jesus in Matthew. Are you in need of guidance and rest? READ ON! God had a plan for His scattered sheep! And this is it.

Religion without Jesus is a hopeless endeavor that is sure to bring heavy burdens, weariness, anxiety, and an overall darkness.

Bad shepherds versus the Good Shepherd

Weariness of soul is not just that a person is overworked and tired. It is the dryness that a fruitless and joyless religion brings to the core of our being. Religion without Jesus is a hopeless endeavor that is sure to bring heavy burdens, weariness, anxiety, and an overall darkness. And God is not happy with this type of religious leadership either, and He exposes it in detail and in no uncertain terms:

"Son of man, prophesy against the shepherds of Israel. Prophesy and say to those shepherds, 'Thus says the Lord GOD, "Woe, shepherds of Israel who have been feeding themselves! Should not the shepherds feed the flock? You eat the fat and clothe yourselves with the wool, you slaughter the fat sheep without feeding the flock. Those who are sickly you have not strengthened, the diseased you have not healed, the broken you have not bound up, the scattered you have not brought back, nor have you sought for the lost; but with force and with severity you have dominated them. . . . My flock wandered through all the mountains and on every high hill; My flock was scattered over all the surface of the earth, and there was no one to search or seek for them." ' "

" ' ". . . Behold, I am against the shepherds, and I will demand My sheep from them. . . ." ' "

. . . "Behold, I Myself will search for My sheep and seek them out. As a shepherd cares for his herd in the day when he is among his scattered sheep, so I will care for My sheep and will deliver them from all the places to which they were scattered on a cloudy and gloomy day" (Ezekiel 34:2–6, 10–12).

God is not happy with the way His sheep have been treated! And what a warning to all of us who shepherd His sheep! Scattered, dominated, oppressed, and abandoned sheep—this was **not what God had in mind!!**

The last occurrence of the verb *"give rest"* in the first-person singular, future tense, in the Septuagint comes right after this prophecy against the shepherds of Israel: " 'I will feed My flock and I will lead them to rest [I will give rest—*anapausō*],' declares the Lord GOD" (verse 15). **How will He do** such a thing? I am SO glad you asked! "Then I will set over them one shepherd, My servant David, and he will feed them; he will feed them himself and be their shepherd. . . . Then they will know that I am the LORD, when I have broken the bars of their yoke and have delivered them from the hand of those who enslaved them" (verses 23, 27). Woo-hoo! Woo-hoo! Woo-hoo!

At the time when God sent this word to the prophet, David had been dead for many years. God is talking here about David's descendant, the Davidic Shepherd Prince, Jesus, who would come to *give rest* to His sheep. WOW! This is too good! Let's take a moment to summarize Ezekiel 34.

God will rescue His sheep (Israel) from the false

shepherds, and He Himself will search for them (verses 10, 11) and care for them (verses 12, 13). The end result will be rest: "They will *rest* in perfect prosperity" (verse 14, LXX). The promise that follows comes from the mouth of God Himself: "I will feed my sheep and *I will give rest* [*anapausō*] to them" (verse 15, LXX), echoing the psalmist's portrayal of the Lord as his Shepherd, who takes him to green grass and waters of rest (*anapausis*) in Psalm 23:2. This time the enemies of Israel, from whom God will give them *rest,* are their own "shepherds" and through His future Davidic prince, God will break the bars of their oppressive "yoke" (Ezekiel 34:27).

It is very important to understand the relationship between God's promise of rest, mediated through the future Davidic King and the breaking of the oppressive yoke of the shepherds because it is an integral part of the promise of Jesus in Matthew 11:28–30. The hope of the Messianic rest finds fulfillment when the "one" Davidic Shepherd King reigns over them (Ezekiel 34:23, 24). God's "giving of rest" is therefore mediated by the divine representative, the future Davidic King. Perhaps you want to take a moment to read all of Ezekiel 34, which is one of the most passionate chapters in Scripture where God promises to take care of His weary sheep.

I Will Give You *Rest*

I will give rest!

There are times when we are all weary and tired of the burdens of life. But no fatigue is worse than the weariness that results from carrying the yoke of a Christ-less religion, like the one proposed and portrayed by the Pharisees (read Matthew 12:1–14). In that religious framework, the *Sabbath rest* that was designed to point to the identity and mission of Jesus as the new Moses and promised Davidic King, and to remind us to *rest* in the reality that our Creator is also our Redeemer, becomes a heavy burden instead.

> *J*esus wanted to offer *His rest* to the weary soul.

Jesus wanted to offer *His rest* to the weary soul. The Sabbath rest was designed to remind us about that reality on a weekly basis so that we would never forget the Creator-Redeemer. He is the ONLY One who can assure us: "I will give you *Sabbath rest* for your soul" (see Matthew 11:28, 29). I pray that these few findings that I have shared with you will help you to discover a new and deeper *rest* in the reality of redemption provided by Jesus and celebrated on the seventh day of the week, the day of completion and freedom.

Now, please place your name in the blank spaces, in place of the pronouns *me, my,* and *I,* and celebrate the full meaning of these verses:

Rest in Jesus' Promise!!

The Lord is _____*'s shepherd, and* _____*shall lack nothing. He makes* _____ *lie down in green pastures; He leads*_____ *beside waters of rest [anapausis]. He restores* _____*'s soul. (Psalm 23:1–3; author's translation and paraphrase).*

1. For a complete academic version of the PhD dissertation, please contact the author through the ministry Web site: www .Jesus101.tv.

2. For an academic rendering of this topic, please see Elizabeth Talbot, "Rest, Eschatology and Sabbath in Matthew 11:28–30: An Investigation of Jesus' Offer of Rest in the Light of the Septuagint's Use of *Anapausis*," in Craig A. Evans and H. Daniel Zacharias, eds., *"What Does the Scripture Say?" Studies in the Function of Scripture in Early Judaism and Christianity* (London: T&T Clark, 2012), 57–69.

3. Josephus, *Against Apion 2,* 174.

CHAPTER 5

REST in Jesus' RESTORATION!!

"Help me, I'm Amanda Berry."

With one frantic 911 call on Monday evening, three women missing for years were found in a Cleveland house where they had been held against their will by three brothers, police in Ohio said.

"I've been kidnapped," Berry, who disappeared a decade ago, told the dispatcher. "I've been missing for 10 years and I'm out here. I'm free now.". . .

Berry and two other women, Gina DeJesus and Michelle Knight, went missing between 2000 and 2004 in separate incidents. The women were all between the ages of 14 and 20 when they vanished. . . .

"The nightmare is over," said Cleveland FBI Special Agent in Charge Stephen Anthony. "These three young ladies have provided us with the ultimate definition of survival and perseverance. The healing can now begin."

Authorities said they never stopped looking for the missing women, running down tips and even digging up two backyards. The break came when Berry summoned the courage to escape. . . .

Shocked relatives could hardly believe that their missing family members had been found after so many years.[1]

During those ten years, these three young women didn't have a single day of *complete rest*. They were captives, held against their will, in a place not of their own choosing, and yearning to go home. I am so happy that they eventually were restored to their families and to a life of normalcy, even though they probably still have nightmares every once in a while. I can't even imagine what they must have gone through. Their only hope was to trust that there was a way to get out, that someone was still looking for them, and that this was not the end of their story. They surrounded themselves with mental and written visualizations of who they were and what they hoped for. And those beliefs kept them alive.

You and I may not have been kidnapped, but all of us have been through some other very difficult experience, such as divorce, addiction, depression, or being financially destitute. Maybe your kids are in trouble or you are worried about your future, in terms of education, employment, relationships, or retirement. Perhaps you have lost a loved one and are now in deep mourning. Perchance this book finds you dealing with some really bad news about your health. Your friends may have betrayed you and you may feel very much alone, without anyone who seems to understand or even care. Perhaps simply tuning in to TV news gives you a bad adrenaline rush, and in the very core of your soul you feel that this is not your home.

You were made for peace and not for anxiety. You were created for abundance and not for pain; you have been designed for life and not for death!

You were made for peace and not for anxiety. You were created for abundance and not for pain; you have been designed for life and not for death! Humans were made in the image of God, and "He has also set eternity in their heart" (Ecclesiastes 3:11). This is why there is this constant nagging feeling in the core of our souls that reminds us that this world is not our home. And we get *restless*. . .

We all have been kidnapped by an evil villain who stands against peace and joy. From the beginning of our story, the adversary of God stood against the perfect life God had created for His children (take a moment to read about the beginning of pain and death in this world in

I Will Give You *Rest*

Genesis 3) and thought he had gotten away with it. **But he did not!** (See Genesis 3:15.)

God vowed to get us back, even though it would cost Him His own life! He paid the ransom and promised to come back for His kidnapped children. In the mean-

Yes! It is true! Believe it! We are going home!!

while, as we wait for His return, the only way to have *complete rest* in our souls is to be assured of His promises, believing that what He said is TRUE, and that what He DID is fully sufficient for our salvation. Take a moment to read Jesus' words out loud: "Do not let your heart be troubled; believe in God, believe also in Me. In My Father's house are many dwelling places; if it were not so, I would have told you; for I go to prepare a place for you. If I go and prepare a place for you, I will come again and receive you to Myself, that where I am, there you may be also" (John 14:1–3).

Yes! It is true! Believe it! **We are going home**!!

The *best* is yet to come!

I am sure you've heard this story before, because it is all over the Internet. In this section, I will use John Ortberg's version:[2]

Rest in Jesus' Restoration!!

I read recently about a woman who had been diagnosed with cancer and was given three months to live. Her doctor told her to make preparations to die, so she contacted her pastor and told him how she wanted things arranged for her funeral service—which songs she wanted to have sung, what Scriptures should be read, what words should be spoken—and that she wanted to be buried with her favorite Bible. But before he left, she called out to him, *"One more thing."*

"What?"

"This is important. I want to be buried with a fork in my right hand." The pastor did not know what to say. No one had ever made such a request before. So she explained. "In all my years going to church functions, whenever food was involved, my favorite part was when whoever was cleaning dishes of the main course would lean over and say, *You can keep your fork.*

"It was my favorite part because I knew that it meant something great was coming. It wasn't Jell-O. It was something with substance—cake or pie—biblical food.

"So I just want people to see me there in my casket with a fork in my hand, and I want them to wonder, *What's with the fork?* Then I want you to tell them, *Something better is coming. Keep your fork.*"

As I mentioned, you probably have heard this story before. I have frequently included it in my sermons. But this story became particularly important for me because of my mom. She had heard me tell this story many times. One day, when I was gone, preaching out of state, she called me on the phone while on her way to the emergency room. She told me that she wasn't feeling well because her cancer was advancing rapidly and that she and my dad were heading to the hospital. And then, in her always cheerful and enthusiastic way, she added, "But don't worry, I am holding a fork in my hand!" I will never forget her words. She passed away a few weeks later.

> *I* think it all boils down to this: believing that the **best** is yet to come!

What does it take for a person to live or die with a fork in his or her hand? I think it all boils down to this: believing that the **best** is yet to come!

God decided to reveal to us the end of the redemption story. He is coming back for us, and He will **restore** all things! And this is the only way to live a *restful, sabbathed* life in the midst of terrorist attacks, tornadoes, and bad news: Christ, our Righteousness, is **our only hope!** Jesus lived a perfect life, died in our place, and victoriously resurrected from the dead! That is why we live with a fork in our hands, assured that *the best* is yet to come! We can live (or die) in complete *rest,* not because of who we are, but because of who He is, and what He has done!

Tears turned to joy!

The second coming of Jesus is the great hope of the Christian faith.[3] Having died in His first advent in order to pay the ransom for humanity, Christ comes a second time to take us to be with Him forever. It means to receive the hug of our Creator we have been waiting for. It means the end of pain and death. It means to be with our Beloved, once again, as in the beginning. The description of Jesus' triumphant return is breathtaking. (Take a moment to read Revelation 19:11–13.)

The signs of the coming of Christ were never meant to frighten us but to encourage us. I still remember a small group where we were discussing how the signs of His coming are like points in a map that reveal that the destination is growing closer. A wonderfully positive woman shared an insight that I will never forget. She told the group that when her children

> The signs of the coming of Christ were never meant to frighten us but to encourage us.

were young, they loved to visit their grandparents, and they had learned different landmarks along the way to know that they were getting closer. As they recognized these signs, they grew more and more excited, knowing that their much-awaited encounter with their beloved grandparents was at hand. Then she concluded, "This is the role of the signs of the second coming of Jesus. They are there so that we may recognize His closeness and get more and more excited!" I believe this with all my heart!

Even to the first generation of Christians, who almost two thousand years ago saw Jesus taken to heaven in front of their eyes, the news of Jesus' second coming was given as a source of hope and joy: "And after He had said these things, He was lifted up while they were looking on, and a cloud received Him out of their sight. And as they were gazing intently into the sky while He was going, behold, two men in white clothing stood beside them. They also said, 'Men of Galilee, why do you stand looking into the sky? This Jesus, who has been taken up from you into heaven, will come in just the same way as you have watched Him go into heaven' " (Acts 1:9–11).

This promise of another coming of Jesus became known as the *parousia,* and it set the Christian community afire.

One of the most noticeable characteristics of those waiting for Jesus will be their rejoicing with the

Bridegroom (Jesus). Exploring the parable of the ten virgins (see Matthew 25:1–13), one of my favorite authors ends her comments with a description of the amazing, indescribable rejoicing of that awaited encounter:

To His faithful followers Christ has been a daily companion and familiar friend. They have lived in close contact, in constant communion with God. Upon them the glory of the Lord has risen. In them the light of the knowledge of the glory of God in the face of Jesus Christ has been reflected. Now they rejoice in the undimmed rays of the brightness and glory of the King in His majesty. They are prepared for the communion of heaven; for they have heaven in their hearts.

With uplifted heads, with the bright beams of the Sun of Righteousness shining upon them, with rejoicing that their redemption draweth nigh, they go forth to meet the Bridegroom, saying, "Lo, this is our God; we have waited for Him, and He will save us" (Isaiah 25:9).

"And I heard as it were the voice of a great multitude, and as the voice of many waters, and as the voice of mighty thunderings, saying, Alleluia; for the Lord God omnipotent reigneth. Let us be glad and rejoice, and give honour to Him; for the marriage of the Lamb is come, and His wife hath made herself ready. . . . And he saith unto me, Write, Blessed are they which are called unto the marriage supper of the Lamb." "He is Lord of lords, and King of kings; and they that are with Him are called, and chosen, and faithful" (Revelation 19:6–9; 17:14).[4]

Yes! Tears turned to **joy!** Hopelessness turned to **peace!** Anxiety turned to **rest!** Death turned to **life!** And the *best* news is that you can start experiencing this *restful reality in Jesus* **today,** and surrendering to it now! That's why Jesus promised *rest for our souls* when we believe in Him (see Matthew 11:28–30)! We start experiencing the eternal realities of heaven already now, while still on this sin-scarred earth. Woo-hoo!

> *Tears turned to joy! Hopelessness turned to peace! Anxiety turned to rest! Death turned to life!*

Rest as eternal peaceful dwellings

A few months ago, in order to save money, our ministry, Jesus 101 Biblical Institute (www.jesus101.tv), relocated to Riverside, California. The cost of living at our new location is much lower in comparison with the area where our offices were located before. As the moving plans got underway, I suddenly realized that my salary would go down significantly as well. I discussed it with my husband, and we prayed about it and decided to trust that God would give us a peaceful home at the new location with a much lower mortgage payment than before, so that we could afford it with the new lower salary. Then the most amazing thing happened! We believe it was a miracle! We found a brand-new house in a gated community, with miles of walking trails and many amenities to enjoy. It is a small house, and yet it has everything we need and more! As I sit by the window writing this book, I am looking at the gorgeous mountain view and lush greenery that God has gifted us with. And all of this for a little over one-third of what we used to pay before! Every morning, we are still in awe of the peaceful dwelling God had prepared for us long before we even knew we needed it!

All of us want to live in a peaceful, restful place. This is why it is very important to notice that, as we continue the *anapausis* (*rest*) word study in the Greek Old Testament (which we touched upon in the previous chapter), we find that in the prophetic books of the LXX the most prominent meaning of this word is *a peaceful dwelling,* not just on this earth, but *the eternal restful and peaceful dwellings* promised for the people of God.

I Will Give You *Rest*

For example, Isaiah contains twenty-nine instances of *anapausis* and its word-group, the most occurrences of any book in the LXX.[5] Of these occurrences, some two-thirds are used with the clear meaning of "dwelling" or "settling." The emphasis is placed on the dwelling place, not just on the absence of enemies, but on the actual possession and/or inheritance of their own land as a final resting place. This meaning spills over to many other prophetic books. And this is a prominent background to be added to Jesus' promise in Matthew 11:28, 29: "Come to Me, all who are weary and heavy-laden, and I will give you *rest*. Take My yoke upon you . . . and **you will find *rest* for your souls**" (emphasis added).

Jesus would come as the promised Davidic Prince and *give rest* (*anapausō*) to His scattered sheep (see Ezekiel 34:15), "so that they may live securely in the wilderness and sleep in the woods" (verse 25). I think that it is not a coincidence that Psalm 23:1–3 (Psalm 22:1–3, LXX) uses the same word to visualize a peaceful dwelling. Let's read it out loud:

The Lord is my shepherd, I shall not be in need.
He makes me lie down in green pastures;
He leads me beside waters of rest [*anapausis*].
He restores my soul (author's translation).

Rest in Jesus' Restoration!!

Yes! We all want a *restful dwelling place*. Forever. But how do we experience these eternal realities now, in this world, where Jesus already confirmed that we will have trouble? I am SO glad you asked. This is a core question! And Jesus Himself gave the answer: "These things I have spoken to you, so that *in Me* you may have peace. In the world you have tribulation, but take courage; *I have overcome the world*!" (John 16:33; emphasis added).

> The Creator is also the Redeemer and the Re-Creator.

When we accept the invitation to come to Jesus (Matthew 11:28–30), we choose to believe that He is reliable, trustworthy, faithful, and powerful to bring us to an *eternal, restful dwelling,* which He had designed from the beginning of humankind. The Creator is also the Redeemer and the Re-Creator. This eternal reality becomes the core of our existence, and our soul is in complete *rest.* We come to believe in that "end of the story," which has already been revealed to us in the Bible. *Rest is not* the absence of trouble but the *presence of the Restorer!*

Re-creation

And the day is coming, when the earth will be re-created and will become the new earth (see Revelation

21). It is very significant that our permanent home will be the same place where we were at the beginning, because this was one of the roles of the kinsman-redeemer (see chapter 2 in this book). Remember how he had to redeem property that was given up by a poor relative? "If a fellow countryman of yours becomes so poor he has to sell part of his property, then his nearest kinsman [*go'el*] is to come and buy back what his relative has sold" (Leviticus 25:25). Jesus, our Kinsman-Redeemer, not only rescued us through the ransom He paid, but He also got our land back (the earth) as well! The Bible comes full circle through the blood of the Lamb!

As we open the book of Revelation, we immediately get into the language that was used at the beginning of the Jewish Scriptures; for example, "To him who overcomes, I will grant to eat of the tree of life which is in the Paradise of God" (Revelation 2:7). The tree of life and Paradise are words we encountered in Genesis 2, when God prepared the ultimate "nursery" for His beloved children. The tree of life is also present in Genesis 3, with the sad reminder that humans would no longer have access to it because they were now mortal. But as we get to the place where the cosmic view of Jesus' ministry is unveiled, we start hearing this type of language again.

When we start reading Revelation 21, John announces that he "saw a new heaven and a new earth; . . . and there is no longer any sea" (verse 1). For the first-century Mediterranean world, the sea was the place where evil resided. Evil is no more. And a loud voice from the throne is heard. This voice announces the fulfillment of the ongoing covenant theme that was spoken at different times and in different ways all through the Bible, always pointing to God dwelling with His people (verses 3, 4).

> The presence of God with His people has been the theme throughout the history of humankind

The presence of God with His people has been the theme throughout the history of humankind. They were created to be with Him. We are reminded of this throughout the Old Testament. "I will make My dwelling among you. . . . I will also walk among you and be your God, and you shall be My people" (Leviticus 26:11, 12). Moreover, God designed a way in which His people would experience His presence: the tabernacle in the wilderness and, eventually, the temple. God manifested the glory of His presence in these sacred structures.

When Jesus became flesh, He *tabernacled* (it is the same word as *tabernacle* only in a verb form, usually translated as "dwelt") among us, and once again "we saw His glory, glory as of the only begotten from the Father, full of grace and truth" (John 1:14). Jesus was the ultimate representation of God's glory (Hebrews 1:1–3). In the new earth, the tabernacle of God is among men because He is dwelling with them forevermore. There is no more temple because God Himself is among them: "I saw no temple in it, for the Lord God the Almighty and the Lamb are its temple" (Revelation 21:22).

God is finally back with His children, whom He lost in Paradise. The covenant of God was given to Adam, Noah, Abraham, Moses, and David in the Jewish Scriptures. These men of old received signs of the covenant and had glimpses of its developmental nature (see the analysis of this concept in chapters 1 and 3 of this book). When we get to the new earth, the covenant will be fulfilled and the ultimate reality for us will be that we will have received the **divine sonship.** We are, in fact, children of God! God will be with us, and we will be with God! Reunited! Forever! The accomplishment of this final reality will be announced by God Himself (see verse 21:7).

Let's pause for a moment to internalize this ultimate *reality of an eternal, restful dwelling* with God. Fill in the blanks with your name:

> *Then _____ saw a new heaven and a new earth; for the first heaven and the first earth passed away . . . . And _____ heard*

a loud voice from the throne, saying, "Behold, the tabernacle of God is among men, and He will dwell among them, and they shall be His people, and God Himself will be among them" (verses 1–3),

The last book of the Bible ends with a scene of the redeemed humanity, returned to the tree of life. We have come full circle: "Then he showed me a river of the water of life, clear as crystal, coming from the throne of God and of the Lamb, in the middle of its street. On either side of the river was the tree of life, bearing twelve kinds of fruit, yielding its fruit every month; and the leaves of the tree were for the healing of the nations" (Revelation 22:1, 2).

The same tree that God planted in Paradise in the beginning is back. Remember how Jesus promised Paradise to the criminal on the cross (Luke 23:43)? Here we are, standing by the tree of life again. Then John utters the seventh and last beatitude in his book: "Blessed are those *who wash their robes,* so that they may have the right to the tree of life, and may enter by the gates into the city" (Revelation 22:14; emphasis added).

The expression of "wash[ing] their robes" has already been explained previously in Revelation: "They have *washed their robes* and made them white in the blood of the Lamb" (Revelation 7:14; emphasis added). Those who are now the blessed ones have the right to the tree of life, a symbol of immortality, because they have washed their robes in the blood of the Lamb; they accepted the ransom paid by their *Go'el*. This is the only reason why they have the right to go back to the tree of life, which

This is our final and eternal, peaceful dwelling of rest.

humans lost when they followed the kidnapper. And this is *our final and eternal, peaceful dwelling of rest.*

The weekly *sabbatical feast of remembrance* was created by God for humans (see Mark 2:27) so that we would constantly celebrate (and never forget) that our Creator is also our Re-Creator, and therefore our souls may be at *rest*. We will continue celebrating and worshiping our Creator, Redeemer, and Re-Creator for eternity!

"For just as the new heavens and the new earth
Which I make will endure before Me," declares the
    Lord,
"So your offspring and your name will endure.
"And it shall be from new moon to new moon
And from *sabbath to sabbath,*
All mankind will come to bow down before Me," says
    the Lord (Isaiah 66:22, 23; emphasis added).

Rest in Jesus' Restoration!!

Complete *rest*!

A few years ago, the theme of *complete rest in Christ* literally took over my life. Perhaps it was because I went through some really dark times in my life or because I witnessed a "divine reversal," where God turned challenges into blessings for myself and others (Romans 8:28). I had not expected to lose my mom to cancer, and this theological theme, running from Genesis to Revelation, became a lifesaver for me. During the past decade, I embarked on an academic journey as I immersed myself in this overarching biblical theology of *rest in Christ*. (My mom got to enjoy the completion of my PhD on the subject, and, in her funny style, wore my graduation gown and gave her own graduation speech for my family, making us laugh until our stomachs hurt! And it is all caught on video!)

As I studied this subject in depth, I started to connect the dots. I gained new understanding and discovered the real meaning of many of the things that I had observed since my childhood, among them the reason for the *weekly sabbatical rest, the rest in Christ when we die, and the eternal restful life that He has assured for us*. The Scriptures became like a well for me, and the deeper I delved into it, the more vividly I understood that all the doctrines and biblical principles lead me to the source of living water: Jesus' victory on the cross on my behalf, and the *rest* for my soul that results thereof.

Consequently, what I discovered ceased to be only doctrines, principles, or beliefs. Instead, it became the reason why, in spite of all the troubles, I could live in this world, day by day, with complete peace and with no anxiety. I am absolutely sure that my dear Savior is reliable and trustworthy, powerful and truthful, and that even when I can't understand everything from my point of view, I can still live *in complete rest* because the Creator's hands were nailed to the cross, giving me the assurance of salvation and restoration.

> *I* could live in this world, day by day, with complete peace and with no anxiety.

The identity and mission of Jesus is the embodiment and fulfillment of the upcoming eschatological (end times or eternal) Messianic *rest,* remembered and celebrated weekly on the *Sabbath day of rest.* Jesus' promise and offer of *anapausis (rest)* is an eternal reality experienced already now, in the heart of each person who heeds the invitation of Jesus (Matthew 11:28–30). It causes an inner repose brought about by the assurance in Christ, a *sabbath rest for the soul,* offered by Jesus, who is the new and greater Moses. It introduces a present eschatological and eternal *rest* experienced within as an appetizer of things to come, brought about by the divine Davidic Shepherd King, who is the King of kings and the Lord of lords (Revelation 19:11–16).

I really wanted to find an image that would capture this experience and theological theme. How can one express the words of Jesus, **"I will give you rest"** in a drawing or painting? Then I found a piece of artwork. For several years, I constantly had it with me and kept looking at it. However, the problem was that I could not find the artist of the painting. I am SO thankful to the Pacific Press® Publishing Association because they took the time to find the artist and purchased the right to use this awesome visualization on the cover of this book. Every detail touches my heart: Jesus fully embracing the little girl, as she has found *complete rest* in His arms. His passionate expression, being reunited with His child. The girl's *restful* facial expression, as she finally is able *to rest* from anxiety and troubles, safe in her Rescuer's embrace. Her hand grabbing His shoulder, never to let go, never to return to the evil kidnapper, *resting* in complete trust and assurance.

Come to Me, and I will give you rest!

Everything in this painting summarizes the whole plan of redemption: **Come to Me, and I will give you rest!**

I Will Give You *Rest*

The Bible ends with this invitation, with the Spirit and the church joining in! "The Spirit and the Bride say, 'Come.' And let the one who hears say, 'Come.' And let the one who is thirsty come; let the one who wishes take the water of life without cost" (Revelation 22:17).

I pray that you will accept the invitation of Jesus to *rest* in His Victory, Faithfulness, Provision, Promise, and Restoration. Only at the cross will you find *His True Rest*. He has made a promise regarding our past, our present, and our future: "**You will find rest for your souls**" (Matthew 11:29).

And I believe Him with all my heart! Do you?

Take a deep breath, and enter *His rest*!

Already! Now!

Woo-hoo!!

1. "Three Ohio Women Found Alive After Being Missing for a Decade; 3 Men Arrested," NBC News, May 6, 2013, http://usnews.nbcnews.com/_news/2013/05/06/18091211-three-ohio-women-found-alive-after-being-missing-for-a-decade-3-men-arrested?lite.

2. John Ortberg, *If You Want to Walk on Water, You've Got to Get Out of the Boat* (Grand Rapids, MI: Zondervan, 2004), 169, 170.

3. Parts of this section are further discussed in Elizabeth Viera Talbot's book, *Surprised by Love: A 10-Week Bible Study Series for Women* (Nampa, ID: Pacific Press® Publishing Association, 2013), 78–90.

4. Ellen G. White, *Christ's Object Lessons* (Washington, DC: Review and Herald® Publishing Association, 1941), 421.

5. For an academic rendering of this topic, please see Talbot, "Rest, Eschatology and Sabbath in Matthew 11:28–30," in Evans and Zacharias, eds., *What Does the Scripture Say?* 57–69.

*F*or additional FREE resources, videos on demand, daily devotionals, biblical studies, audio books, and much more, please visit our Web site:

www.Jesus101.tv

If you have been blessed by this booklet and would like to help us keep spreading the good news of Jesus Christ through preaching, teaching, and writing, please send your donations to

Jesus 101 Biblical Institute
P. O. Box 10008
San Bernardino, CA 92423

WATCH the JESUS 101
channel on ROKU!

DOWNLOAD the
JESUS 101 app TODAY!